WRITING INTERSECTIONAL IDENTITIES

WRITING INTERSECTIONAL IDENTITIES

Keywords for Creative Writers

**JANELLE ADSIT
AND RENÉE M. BYRD**

BLOOMSBURY ACADEMIC
LONDON • NEW YORK • OXFORD • NEW DELHI • SYDNEY

BLOOMSBURY ACADEMIC
Bloomsbury Publishing Plc
50 Bedford Square, London, WC1B 3DP, UK
1385 Broadway, New York, NY 10018, USA

BLOOMSBURY, BLOOMSBURY ACADEMIC and the Diana logo
are trademarks of Bloomsbury Publishing Plc

First published in Great Britain 2019

Cover design: Eleanor Rose
Cover image © Getty Images

Bloomsbury Publishing Plc does not have any control over, or responsibility
for, any third-party websites referred to or in this book. All internet addresses given in
this book were correct at the time of going to press. The author and publisher regret
any inconvenience caused if addresses have changed or sites have ceased to exist,
but can accept no responsibility for any such changes.

A catalogue record for this book is available from the British Library.

Library of Congress Cataloging-in-Publication Data
Names: Adsit, Janelle, author. | Byrd, Renée M., author.
Title: Writing Intersectional Identities : Keywords for Creative Writers /
Janelle Adsit and Renée M. Byrd.
Description: London ; New York, NY : Bloomsbury Academic, 2019. |
Includes bibliographical references.
Identifiers: LCCN 2018057052 | ISBN 9781350065734 (hb) | ISBN 9781350065727 (pb) |
ISBN 9781350065741 (epub) | ISBN 9781350065758 (ePDF)
Subjects: LCSH: Identity (Psychology) in literature–Terminology. | Authorship–Technique.
Classification: LCC PN56.I42 A37 2019 | DDC 808.06/63–dc23 LC record
available at https://lccn.loc.gov/2018057052

ISBN: HB: 978-1-3500-6573-4
         PB: 978-1-3500-6572-7
         ePDF: 978-1-3500-6575-8
         eBook: 978-1-3500-6574-1

Typeset by Integra Software Services Pvt. Ltd.
Printed and bound in Great Britain

To find out more about our authors and books visit www.bloomsbury.com
and sign up for our newsletters.

CONTENTS

ACKNOWLEDGMENTS

In an individualistic society, such as our own, writers are encouraged to highlight the uniqueness of their voices and contributions. However, our ideas are never individually wrought. They are forged in community. That is particularly true with a volume such as this. It attempts to cover a wide terrain. Over and over again throughout the writing, we have marveled at how meeting the challenge of each keyword reminded us of all the great teachers we have learned from in our time in universities and outside of them. As Renée wrote the entry for diaspora, she couldn't help returning to the profound lessons learned from Dr. Julia Chinyere Oparah in the Ethnic Studies Department at Mills College. Janelle appreciated all she owes Conchitina Cruz as she wrote so many entries; Conchitina's scholarship and conversation have been a continuous gift. We become who we are and gain a critical vocabulary for understanding power in community and in struggle.

We would like to thank our editors at Bloomsbury, David Avital, Clara Herberg, and Lucy Brown. Thanks to David for having the idea for this book and for trusting us with it, and to the team at Bloomsbury for shepherding this book into being. We would also like to thank Kelley Ellion and Moxie Alvarez for editorial support. We have so much gratitude for the writers who we cite throughout this text. Please note that the third-party copyrighted materials displayed in the pages of this book are done so on the basis of "fair use for the purposes of teaching, criticism, scholarship or research" only in accordance with international copyright laws, and are not intended to infringe upon the ownership rights of the original owners.

Thanks go to our colleagues at Humboldt State University, especially Christina Accomando, Janet Winston, Barbara Curiel, Andrea Juarez, Kirby Moss, Kumi Watanabe-Schock, Jay Schock, and Sarah Jaquette Ray, for their friendship and shared conversation. Thanks also to the College of Arts, Humanities and Social Sciences for commitment to our scholarship.

For Janelle, profound thanks go to Eric and Lisa Adsit, who have read things they never thought they would be reading—thank you for the gift of your time, care, confidence, and encouragement. Deep gratitude also goes to John Johnson who should be cited on almost every page of this and the other books I've written. You've taught me what it means to feel it in my bones.

For Renée, a debt of gratitude is owed to Margo Okazawa-Rey, Julia Chinyere Oparah, Ajuan Mance, Cynthia Chandler, Tani Barlow, Marcia Byrd, and all of the other great women who've believed in me. To my intellectual confidant, Alic Shook, knowing that you are out in the world is a gift of enormous proportions. Loren Cannon, Mira Friedman, Jen Eagan, and Molly Talcott—thank you for letting me be my wild and weird self. This book would not have been possible without the tireless support of Ryan Rasmussen. You are a super soulmate. May we build a world fit for our Íde bear.

Introduction

For Students

Writers contribute to culture. Every time you sit down to write you are at once drawing upon and speaking back to the cultural ideas you know. In other words, we are influenced by culture, as we also influence it.

As a writer, you are representing human beings with diverse identities. The representations you construct may, to varying extents, sustain the status quo or contribute to change. Literature enables us to imagine new worlds; it allows us to envision that things could be otherwise. But to really take hold of this power to envision the alternative, to envision otherwise, we need to understand what *is*—what is our world? As Avery Gordon writes, "We need to know where we live in order to imagine living elsewhere. We need to imagine living elsewhere before we can live there" (2004, 101). This book is meant to help you add depth to your understanding of identity and culture, and the systems of power that mediate them.

How often do you think about the terms that you find in this book's table of contents when you are writing and revising? Some writers have not yet reflected upon how power, identity, and culture figure in their work. Other writers may feel perpetually assaulted by questions about our belonging or authenticity in our writerly craft; some of us may find ourselves in search of new vocabularies for naming that experience.

This book was written with a range of writers in mind. For those who find the list of terms unfamiliar, this book can serve as an introduction; it can point you to the writers and thinkers who can populate your reading lists. For those who do already think regularly about the role of identity in their work, we've done our best to synthesize some of what has been said about the topic, and we invite you to speak back to the texts you'll find cited—to write the craft-criticism that the field of creative writing needs, as accompaniment to the literary texts you produce.

We invite you to read this book up against the stories, essays, poems, and plays you write and read. Go looking for the ways that the key terms figure in your work and the work that exists on your bookshelf or in your local library. What role does race, class, disability, religion, and gender play in your most recent essay, poem, or story? How do you mark identity in the texts you write? What storylines are given to which characters in your work, and what might condition your choices here? Reading across the key terms, you will be better able to find your potential "blank-spots," to use Gloria Anzaldúa's term. These "blank-spots," if left unchecked, can result in stereotypical portrayals of characters that reinforce harmful ideas about people and groups. Our work as writers has real ramifications for lived experience.

What follows is not meant to be a comprehensive survey of critical theory; instead, what this book offers is a concise introduction to some essential ideas. We've selected a subset of terms that help us to think about what it means to write identity. We've purposefully designed the book to be a readable length, as some readers may choose to read the text from front to back. It can also serve as a reference or pocket guide.

There are many ways of reading this book. You can read it from start to finish, or allow one term to lead you to the next in a connective web. Every word is related in some way to every other in this text, and any way you choose to move through the book will reveal links.

Browse the chapters and you may find terms that are familiar to you. However, even if you think you know and understand a term, there may be more to uncover. The words that head each chapter are powerful terms, with many volumes of writing behind them, produced by scholars across countries and generations. The conversations surrounding these terms exceed what we can present in a pocket guide such as this. While it is broader in scope than a dictionary, as it provides elaboration of the debates surrounding a particular term, a keywords book is still a simplification. Our discussions of the terms that you find listed in the table of contents do not provide a complete picture. The chapters in this keywords edition offer instead a basis for doing your own reading and research, to seek out a more nuanced and multidimensional understanding of the concepts presented here.

The words that title each chapter require a learner's stance, one that keeps us ready for new interpretations and new understandings. What these terms have come to mean for creative writers has shifted over time, and these meanings will continue to remain as dynamic as the conversation that surrounds them.

We are conscious that a keywords edition such as this risks being read as the "last word" on a particular topic. What you find in the pages that follow is not an all-encompassing, all-knowing summary of thought. Our goal was not to offer a comprehensive synopsis of all that has been said about a particular word or topic. Rather, we see each installment in this text as provocation—fodder for conversation and further exploration. We write this text with the care and carefulness that seek not to "speak for," but to keep the door open to a conversation that is ongoing, a conversation in which many voices contribute.

And there are many voices in this text. We read scholars, theorists, and creative writers together, knowing that the lines have always been blurred between these roles. We cite amply in order to prompt the writers who use this text to read more. In some ways, *Writing Intersectional Identities* might be better thought of as an index of a kind. The short chapters that follow send readers to many other texts: books published by university presses, works of literature that may show up on a workshop reading list, articles that are available online.

We cite often not to establish a kind of canon; we cite in order to acknowledge who is seated at the table in a discussion of these terms. A canon declares "this is what there is to value," and such a gesture cannot help but reinforce a particular status quo. We like to think of this book, borrowing from Neil Aitken, as a "de-canon" project—one that raises the visibility of writers and ideas that are often left out of often-assigned craft textbooks.

For Instructors

In creative writing, we teach cultural production. Everything that goes on in creative writing—composing a text, revising a text, or discussing a text in workshop—is saturated with questions of identity. Issues of identity are everywhere present in the workshop conversation—in inherited assumptions about authorship, in the cultural traditions that give rise to different genres, in the identity markers writers use in characterization. But writers often lack the tools for talking about these issues in meaningful ways. This collection of keywords opens ways of thinking about identity that promote inclusion and diversity across the creative writing curriculum.

In the wake of much-circulated essays by writers such as Junot Díaz, Claudia Rankine, and Viet Than Nguyen, creative writing has been called to account for its understanding of identity. The critical conversation about creative writing is growing, and with it the awareness of the identity politics at work in the creative writing workshop. This book is an accessible way into these conversations for our students. The ultimate goal of this book is to help students think more critically about what they write and what they say in workshop, as this book also helps students enter and contribute to analytical conversations about literary art-making. The keywords together provide an intersectional lens that we can bring to both the writing desk and the workshop table.

Rather than presenting students with a formula for how to write well, this text offers a heuristic approach to engaging some irresolvable debates and continual considerations in creative writing. Gaining a vocabulary for talking about these key issues, students will be able to write with a broader awareness of how their texts may operate in the world—and who stands to gain or lose from a particular representation.

Crafted to be equally appropriate for the intermediate creative writing workshop and the comprehensive exam list for an MFA program, this book is intended to be a "pocket guide." Specially tailored for the creative writer, each chapter summarizes critical scholarship surrounding a particular term, aiming to give students a sufficient basis for adding this lexicon to their vocabulary. Reading across the chapters, students come to gain a sense of key debates and ideas about identity in creative writing. Encouraging further exploration and study, the bibliography at the back of the book provides suggestions for additional reading.

The book is meant to provide a shared language for the workshop conversation. Designed to be a reference guide that can be kept close at hand, writers in the classroom may find themselves referring to a particular entry when they are discussing a particular feature of a text. Our hope is that this book will invite more explicit discussion of race, class, gender, sexuality, and disability in the creative writing workshop. Race, class, gender, sexuality, and disability are always present in a text, but we often shy away from explicit discussions of them. The chapters that follow can open up conversations that might otherwise be avoided in workshop conversation, offering a basis and framework for the conversations. In the chapters that follow, students gain the language to trouble representations of identity, to question appropriative practices, to consider the extent to which a piece reinforces or works against master narratives.

Writing Intersectional Identities can be integrated with an existing syllabus in several ways. It can be assigned reading before the workshop conversation begins. It might also be read concurrently with texts submitted for workshop, as the writing prompts it. Instructors might choose to keep this small handbook on the workshop table as a reminder to consider multiple aspects of representation. We've purposefully limited our references to literary texts in this book so that each chapter can be mobilized in connection with a range of literatures, as a framework for analysis. We expect that the chapters in this book will be paired with a broad and diverse array of literary texts, in order to more fully reveal the concepts discussed in these pages.

Each of the chapters can also easily translate into writing prompts. For example, students might be asked to experiment with appropriation in order to elucidate their own aesthetic principles and ethics surrounding this practice. Students might be asked to write counternarratives in conjunction with the corresponding chapter. Or students might experiment with writing stories, poems, essays, or plays that take a term like "belonging" as a central motif. Students might also write additional entries for this book, asking what terms are left out.

We see this book as part of a larger project of interrogating the inequities and exclusions of creative writing. We've made editorial decisions with this goal in mind. That said, there are limitations of our approach. We both write in English from a US context, and we acknowledge that our points of reference are influenced by this location in the world. Renée is a faculty member in sociology and Janelle is a faculty member in creative writing. We share an interest in the work of feminists of color, and we share an orientation toward social justice. Our orientation shapes what you can find on these pages, but we have also attempted to offer a broad picture of how each term has circulated in an interdisciplinary critical conversation. We invite classroom conversations that identify the contingency of our perspectives; we wish for students to see this text as written by authors with particular subject-positions. We write using the first person, in order to expose this book as authored by human beings with blank-spots of their own. We claim no objectivity—even as we have been diligent in trying to expand our own genealogies of thought in investigating these terms. We are motivated by our anticipation of the robust conversations that can be prompted by a text like this: questions about the politics of our craft and the implications of our representations. These are the conversations that are perhaps most critical to the field of creative writing as it stands today.

Janelle Adsit and Renée M. Byrd

Arcata, CA

September 2018

Appropriation

If "appropriation" means the use of something that is not one's own, then appropriation is all around us. Texts are characterized by "variation, version, interpretation, imitation, proximation, supplement, increment, improvisation, prequel, sequel, continuation, addition, paratext, hypertext, palimpsest, graft, rewriting, reworking, refashioning, re-vision, re-evaluation" (3), to use a list offered by Julie Sanders in the book *Adaptation and Appropriation: The New Critical Idiom*. All texts draw upon other texts to make meaning—a phenomenon that is sometimes referred to as *intertextuality*. Every text is composed by and in a network of other texts; this is the very nature of writing.

As it is a general condition of textuality, appropriation is also deliberately central to some modes of art-making. Rafael Pérez-Torres, in the book *Movements in Chicano Poetry: Against Myths, Against Margins*, observes that "a primary characteristic of Chicano culture remains its ability to move across numerous textual terrains: the ritual, the mythic, the mass cultural, the folkloric, the hyperreal … A strategy of pastiche and appropriation enables this movement" (208). As Pérez-Torres's example illustrates, some aesthetic traditions and orientations make appropriation deliberately central. At the same time, all traditions are characterized by borrowing of some kind.

While appropriation may be commonplace, it is not without complexity. Appropriation concerns relationships among people, and any analysis of social relationships needs an analysis of power. As Bruce Ziff and Pratima V. Rao note in the introduction to the edited collection *Borrowed Power: Essays on Cultural Appropriation*, cultural appropriation can be harmful to the appropriated community when the act diminishes the vibrancy of a culture, when the impact of the appropriation damages a given cultural object or practice, when the appropriation wrongly allows some to benefit to the detriment of others, when stereotypes are reinforced through the act of appropriation, when appropriation constitutes stealing the cultural forms of others for one's own prestige and profit, or when the practice fails to reflect cultural conceptions of rightful use. In short, appropriation is problematic when the writer has a sense of an unfettered right to take, borrow, steal without responsibility for, or consideration of, the effects of their action.

When a writer revisits, reimagines, or rewrites another's story, is the purpose to recover words that have been hidden, dismissed, or overlooked? Or is the purpose only to support one's own creativity? Appropriation can be done as a gesture of reclamation, or as a gesture of taking over. Put another way, appropriation can be done in the interest of something that is beyond the artist—of recovering history, elevating tradition, and so on—or it can be merely a device for the artist's own creative project. The difference has much to do with the writer's relationship to what is being borrowed: Is there deep respect for the work in its full context, with full acknowledgment of history and relationships of power? Or is the work seen as merely material for the taking?

Gloria Anzaldúa, in the introduction to *Making Face, Making Soul*, demonstrates the power of writing that reclaims what has been removed or pushed out. In so doing, she also draws a sharp distinction between appropriation born out of respect and appropriation that is in the service of dominant culture.

> In our *mestizaje* theories we create new categories for those of us left out or pushed out of the existing ones. We recover and examine non-Western aesthetics while critiquing Western aesthetics; recover and examine non-rational modes and 'blanked-out' realities while critiquing rational, consensual reality; recover and examine indigenous languages while critiquing the 'languages' of the dominant culture. And we simultaneously combat the tokenization and appropriation of our literatures and our writers/ artists. (xxvi)

Anzaldúa's words elucidate the difference between appropriation that co-opts and tokenizes, and appropriation that recovers and examines what has been blanked-out, covered over, or subordinated. There is a difference, Anzaldúa notes, between appropriation and proliferation. Specifically, appropriation "steals and harms," while proliferation "helps heal breaches of knowledge" (xxi).

We are often told in creative writing that "good writers steal," without acknowledging the political questions at stake in this idea. The imperative to "make it new" may motivate some writers to take whatever they can find for their work, with no obligation to consider the ramifications. Doris Sommer notes a "cannibalistic" tendency that is embedded in these common ideas about art-making: Quoting Oswald de Andrade, Sommer summarizes the tendency that "I am only interested in what does not belong to me. Law of Man. Law of the Cannibals." This tendency Sommer, following de Andrade, attributes to a colonial mentality: "Appropriation of the other is what our New World cultures feed on" (11). Sommer continues, "Devouring alterity is what makes us modern (or just human, for Freud), as we participate in an Occidental culture nourished on novelty" (11); Sommer is here noting a Western tendency to fetishize and devour the other under the rubric of the "new."

When the imperative to "make it new" becomes the primary consideration, the potential harms of one's practice often go unchecked. Consider for example the potential harms of making use of a story with limited understanding of its cultural significance or the cultural practices surrounding rightful use. Lenore Keeshig-Tobias writes in the essay "Stop Stealing Native Stories": "Stories are power. They reflect the deepest, the most intimate perceptions, relationships, and attitudes of a people. Stories show how a people, a culture, thinks. [...] So potent are stories that, in native culture, one storyteller cannot tell another's story without permission."

Warren Cariou's essay "Edgework: Indigenous Poetics as Re-Placement," in the collection *Indigenous Poetics in Canada*, echoes this point about the close relationship between story and identity: Quoting Louise Halfe's discussion of her book *Blue Marrow*, Cariou writes of "Cree-ing," which "is the pronunciation of identity, an assertion that the speaker is connected to her people, to a way of life that is larger than herself." Cariou continues, explaining how essential it is to understand story as tied to community: "I think each Indigenous nation expresses its identity and its uniqueness in a similarly active and verbal way. Poetry as a cry, a *cri*, that echoes through communities and through the land itself" (32). While poetry may transcend cultural specificity, "moving across the lines of class and race and epistemology toward something more elemental in us all, something that we feel in our bodies like the sound of a drum" (32), it also takes its power from the connection to culture, community, and land. Poetry and story are based in community and place; to extract a story and appropriate it as one's own, without acknowledging its lineage and its ties to community, is to reduce that story.

When a piece is divorced from its lineage and its tie to community, there is the risk of misrepresenting. Keeshig-Tobias warns the writer who wants to adopt the stories of Indigenous peoples, stories that are not the writer's own: "If you want to write our stories, then be prepared to live with us. And not just for a few months."

Anzaldúa interrogates writers (white writers in particular) who displace the Native writer and appropriate the culture instead of proliferating information about it (xxi). She identifies the breach and misdeed that take place when the writer "'rips off' people of color, examining Native spirituality and myth with a white collector's mentality. She [the white writer] passes off fiction as fact and distorts the true picture of native peoples in a way that they, as writers would not" (xxi).

Anzaldúa's observation prompts us to ask important questions of ourselves, interrogating our motives as artists. We can ask ourselves: Who is this writing for? Whom or what does this writing serve? How would the person I am representing here feel about the work I am doing? Am I writing *about* another, or *for another*? Have I done immersive and intensive research that has prompted me to come to terms with my assumptions, to destabilize the inherited ideas I have? In my research, have I moved beyond learning *about* to come to learn *from*, without demanding that a person become my informant? Have I been open to the question of whether or not this is a responsible project to take on? Have I been willing to set aside my artistic plans in order to understand the potential ramifications of my work?

These are critical questions, and we should not mistake this type of criticality for prohibition. Questioning something is not the same as forbidding or banning it. Claudia Rankine and Beth Loffreda make this point in *The Racial Imaginary*, as they encourage writers to "see if the boundaries of one's imaginative sympathies line up ... with the lines drawn by power" (17). To what extent are your acts of imagination reinforcing or affirming dominant ideas that maintain inequity and oppression? Or does your work disrupt a status quo?

Rankine and Loffreda suggest that we, as writers, come to recognize the limits of our imaginations. Our imaginations are informed by the dominant narratives that we receive in the cultures we are part of. Rankine and Loffreda encourage writers to dwell in the space where we reach our limit: we can "inhabit, as intensely as possible, the moment in which the imagination's sympathy encounters a limit" (17). In this work, there is value in undermining our own sense of authority—our sense of having the "truth," especially the truth about another.

Rankine and Loffreda's recommendations come from the recognition that our imaginations are not our own. Our imaginations are born out of culture: the imagination, "that unknowable portion of the human mind," is, Loffreda and Rankine write, "also a domain of culture—a place crossed up by culture and history, where the conditions in which we were born have had their effect" (21). Here Rankine and Loffreda are questioning the idea that the imagination is a free space—that the imagination is free to make use of whatever it likes, however it likes. This "transcendent" idea of creativity—the idea that imagination is beyond culture and beyond politics—is what Rankine and Loffreda call a "specific and partial" dream that is born of privilege.

M. NourbeSe Philip, in the essay "The Disappearing Debate: Or How the Discussion of Racism Has Been Taken Over by the Censorship Issue," explains how such ideas about the imagination and creativity are tied to privilege: "To state the obvious, in a racist, sexist and classist society, the imagination, if left unexamined, can and does serve the ruling ideas of the time." Philip continues, "The danger with writers carrying their unfettered imaginations into another culture—particularly ... [a] culture which theirs has oppressed and exploited—is that without careful thought, they are likely to perpetuate stereotypical and one-dimensional views of the culture" (103).

Philip's essay addresses the objection that to question the imagination is to censor it. This objection relies upon a gross oversimplification. A check on the imagination is not a type of censorship. It is not censorship to ask if a writer's use of another's story is perpetuating stereotypical and one-dimensional views. It is not censorship to ask questions about a writer's responsibility in the world. It is not censorship to think about the relationship between positionality, power, and privilege, and a person's imagination. It is not censorship to acknowledge, as Philip does, that in an uneven literary playing field—and in a white-centric and inequitable publishing market—white writers "writing about another culture rather than out of it, virtually guarantees that their work will, in a racist society, be received more readily than the work of writers coming from that very culture" (106–107).

Rosemary J. Coombe, in another chapter from the collection *Borrowed Power*, continues this point, noting the problems with the common view that "everyone is implicitly equal in their capacity to write or be written about—to speak or be spoken for." Coombe demonstrates how "such a position purports to be apolitical, but manages only to be ahistorical and blind to relations of power. It ignores the very real social lines along which representation has been structured and the very real difficulties faced by certain social groups to represent themselves and speak on their own behalf" (78).

All of us write in a context of inequity. How we respond to inequities, and how we respond to the political realities of our time, is a matter of responsibility, or what Toni Morrison calls "response-ability." How do we respond to the inequities that characterize our world? How do we foster an ability to respond to each other? In the landmark text and national bestseller *Playing in the Dark: Whiteness and the Literary Imagination*, Morrison launches a theory of reading and writing that entails being aware of "notions of risk and safety" (xi) that are different for each writer. As writers, we make use of other texts. We allude to, cite, reference, call up, and imitate other texts. The spirit in which we do this—and the consciousness we bring to our artistic decisions—matters greatly.

Audience

For whom do you write? This is a question that is sometimes posed in creative writing classes, and finding an answer can be complicated. There are many ways of thinking about audience. Disciplines have approached the study of audience in different ways. Marketing researchers study audience in terms of demographics and target markets. (Note that the term market is used in publishing in different ways, with different meanings: the term "market" may refer to a particular journal or press where a writer may submit their work. The term "market" can also be used as a synonym for a group of anticipated readers or consumers.) Rhetoricians and composition studies researchers such as Lisa Ede and Andrea Lunsford theorize how writers conceive of their intended audience, and how writers invoke an audience. Walter Ong, a historian who studied orality and writing across cultures, has argued that "The Writer's Audience is Always a Fiction," as his famous essay on the topic is titled. Reception studies focuses on how readers read and interpret the text, how readers make use of literature. In reception studies, theorists debate how audiences participate in the co-creation of meaning in relation to texts. Other researchers might examine readerships or groups of people that coalesce around a particular text or genre. One can think of readerships in terms of interpretive communities (a term Stanley Fish used to identify the shared meaning-making that happens among readers of particular texts or genres).

The questions that these different audience researchers ask might include: How do readers choose what to read? How do they discover new books? How do groups of readers, or readerships, coalesce around particular genres or texts? Where do readers find themselves best represented on the page? Many researchers—from both within the publishing industry and outside of it—have been interested in these questions. These questions can be found in books like Evan Brier's *A Novel Marketplace: Mass Culture, the Book Trade, and Postwar American Fiction*, Jim Collins's *Bring on the Books for Everybody: How Literary Culture Become Popular Culture*, Jenny Hartley's *The Reading Groups Book*, and John K. Young's *Black Writers, White Publishers: Marketplace Politics in Twentieth-Century African American Literature*.

There is much existing research on the topic of audience. This research is sometimes left to the side of a creative writing class, however. This choice has a long history arising from a Western aesthetic tradition that defines literature as that which is not directed toward, or co-created with, an audience, but is instead only "overheard" by an audience. In Percy Bysshe Shelley's famous metaphor, articulated in his "Defence of Poetry" (2010): "A Poet is a nightingale, who sits in darkness and sings to cheer its own solitude with sweet sounds." Shelley's nightingale-poet is alone; he is sovereign in his solitude. He has auditors who are "entranced by the melody of an unseen musician, who feel that they are moved and softened, yet know not whence or why." The poet is overheard by an audience, but the poetry is not pronounced for them.

Similarly, J.S. Mill writes, "All poetry is of the nature of soliloquy" (95). This, for Mill, is what differentiates poetry from "eloquence":

> Eloquence is heard; poetry is overheard. Eloquence supposes an audience. The peculiarity of poetry appears to us to lie in the poet's utter unconsciousness of a listener. Poetry is feeling confessing itself to itself in moments of solitude … Eloquence is feeling pouring itself out to other minds, courting their sympathy, or endeavoring to influence their belief, or move them to passion or to action. (95)

In Shelley and Mill, poetry is written for its own sake. Audience, in these conceptions, is an aftereffect of the literary text's coming-into-being.

Creative writers continue to debate the extent to which it is useful to think about audience in the process of writing, but the literary audience is a concern for multiple players in the literary industry. An acquisitions editor thinks about which manuscripts can swiftly reach an audience in order to ensure sales. A literary agent thinks about how to match an author to an audience, using publishing houses as a conduit for making that connection. A publicist thinks about how to identify, or perhaps create, an audience for the writer's work. A promotions team thinks about how to craft marketing strategies that make particular books visible to their intended audiences.

Book proposals and query letters typically include information about target audiences. While writers may choose to compose a text without drawing an explicit picture of their imagined reader, there are often aspects of a text that can point to a most likely reader. Let's say you've written a memoir about growing up in a multigenerational household in Los Angeles. Your memoir is written in Spanish and English, and it focuses on issues of gentrification and cultural ideas about neighborhoods. Now that the manuscript is written, there are some questions to ask yourself to help you identify your target audience:

- What will readers look to your book to find? How are those readers most likely to find or hear about your book?

- What forums (online discussion boards, hashtag feeds, conferences, etc.) are most likely to include a discussion of your book?

- Which books is your book most like? Imagine that there is a thematic display of books in your local library, and your memoir is part of the display. What is the theme of this display, and what other books are included?

- If it's true that we write the books that we want to read, then it stands to reason that we ourselves have some shared characteristics with our intended readers. What are some of those shared characteristics? What about your own interests might be similar to the interests of your intended readers?

To find answers to these questions, you might consult data sources such as the Pew Research Center Book Reading Report or the Association of American Publishers Trade Publishing Report. You might also look for news and figures on book sales and circulation, from sources such as Penguin House's online Author News, or the serial publications *Publishers Marketplace* and *Publishers Weekly*.

Of course, the idea of audience is much more complicated than sales figures. These sales figures emerge from complicated dynamics related to what Barbara Herrnstein Smith calls the "contingencies of evaluation." What literatures are valued (and purchased and read) by different people at different times is a question that is related to every other term we discuss in this book.

Gloria Anzaldúa writes of how she, as a writer of color, had to make space for herself in a literary landscape that prioritized the voices of white writers and male writers. Anzaldúa notes of the contributors to the edited collection *Making Face/Making Soul*, women of color who are poets, novelists, creative nonfiction writers, and scholars: "In addition to the task of writing, or perhaps included in the task for writing, we've had to create a readership and teach it how to 'read' our work" (xviii).

The myth that "there is no audience" for a writer's work is used to silence minoritized writers, or writers whose identities are underrepresented in the industry. Elba Rosario Sánchez writes in the essay "Cartohistografía: Continente de una voz" of the myth of "no audience" that has been used to keep multilingual work from publication: "Despite what many literature profs and editors out there skeptically say," Sánchez writes, "I am confident that there is a significant and, dare I say, large reading audience that is comfortable with an array of *lenguas*" (21).

As Sánchez's example shows, there are power relations at work in our understandings of audience. Considering this, we can reevaluate the idea of a "universal audience." Writers such as Stephen Dobyns in the book *Best Words, Best Order* universalize poetry's audience and use synonymously "the world" and "the reader" when discussing creative writing. This idea of a "universal audience" risks a homogenizing effect that ignores or obfuscates the differences in our identities and the power relations that structure our world. Moreover, the idea of a universalized audience is likely to reinforce a white-centered approach to literature, one that naturalizes as "universal" a specifically white (and heteronormative, upper or middle class, etc.) perspective. Toni Morrison notes this tendency in *Playing in the Dark: Whiteness and the Literary Imagination*: "Until very recently, and regardless of the race of the author, the readers of virtually all of American fiction have been positioned as white" (xii). A supposedly "generic" reader may be implicitly raced—and gendered, classed, etc.—even as these identity categories are neglected or covered over by the idea of a "universal audience."

Dobyns ignores how writing "for 'anyone who reads me'" must be accompanied by an awareness that, in Nadine Gordimer's words from her essay "The Gap between the Writer and Reader," "'anyone' excludes a vast number of readers who cannot 'read' you or me because of concerns they do not share with us in grossly unequal societies" (440). She continues, explaining that "differences [between writer and audience] affect profoundly the imagery, the relativity of values, the referential interpretation of events between the cultural givens of most writers" (444).

Gordimer's point—which asks us to think about difference and the effects of privilege and inequality in textual production (i.e., writers *producing* texts) and textual reception (i.e., readers *receiving* texts)—is echoed by writers and theorists such as Doris Sommer who, in *Proceed with Caution, When Engaged with Minority Writing in the Americas*, critiques the assumption of "cultural continuity" between writer and reader. We should not assume, Sommer writes, that what is true for me is true for another. And as readers we should not assume that we have a full understanding of the texts we encounter. We should read with the cultural humility that acknowledges difference and seeks to learn what is offered, without demanding a certain set of things from the text. This cultural humility follows where the text leads, but does not position a text as a kind of "native informant." Sommer critiques the demand that white readers may place on "minority writing": the demand that the text provide a window into cultural practices for the white gaze, the demand that the text be knowable to the white reader, the demand that the text "speak for" a group.

Sommer and Gordimer help us to question the assumption that one's writing speaks to a "universal" audience that is inclusive of everyone. In Sommer and Gordimer's essays, readers and writers are asked to think about cultural specificity and relations of power, to consider how audiences of differing identities and backgrounds experience each text. Audiences approach texts with different reading practices. We approach the study of audience with awareness of all that is at stake in our conceptions of the reader.

Authenticity

The *Oxford English Dictionary* provides the following definitions for the noun *authenticity*:

1   The fact or quality of being true or in accordance with fact … accurate reflection of real life …

2   … genuineness and

3   … the quality of truthful correspondence between inner feelings and their outward expression

4   … the condition of being true to oneself,

5   the fact or quality of being real; actuality, reality.

Raising questions about the notions of reality, truth, essentialism, and culture, authenticity takes on a host of meanings in the creative writing workshop. A text may be judged based on a criterion of authenticity: "Is the writer sufficiently authentic in this text?," we might ask. The word "authenticity" is readily found in creative writing craft texts. Stephen Minot's book *Three Genres*, for example, warns that if a writer is reluctant to reveal his or her private feelings, "the poem will probably lack a sense of power and authenticity" (136), and this would be to the poem's detriment. Trevor Pateman, in the essay "Writing: Some Thoughts on the Teachable and Unteachable in Creative Writing," describes "finding a voice" as related to, and just as important as, other aesthetic values: specifically, "speaking with a full word sincerely, authentically, and for oneself" (87).

The notion of authenticity opens onto questions about the possibility and nature of a "True Self." The idea of "being true to oneself" is central to modern philosophical thought in the West. Ralph Waldo Emerson extorted us "to be yourself," arguing that to do this "in a world that is constantly trying to make you something else is the greatest accomplishment." But what is this Self? And what does it mean to be "something else?" Symbolic interactionists, such as Erving Goffman, argue that this Self is fashioned from its presentation in everyday life. Many poststructural scholars would argue that there is no essential self. Along those lines, Judith Butler argues that identity is performative. So when it comes to the self, is there no there there? The vexing nature of these questions presents both a challenge and opportunity to creative writers. Perhaps generative writing is in the asking of these questions, rather than in providing answers.

The question of authenticity is bound up with power and agency. If we are to operate with the critique of essentialism presented in other chapters, we must begin to understand authenticity as an open question. If there is no static, inherent characteristic fundamental to a culture or group of people, we have to expect a plurality of diverse experiences. As Homi Bhabha reminds us in *The Location of Culture*, all ideas of an original culture are fictions. A culture is always changing, and hybridity, or cultural influence, is not simply something new inflicted by colonialism and globalization. In fact, through culture, people are always borrowing from new ideas, transforming practices, and making meaning in new ways.

Notions of authenticity are particularly vexing for diasporic writers. In "The Cult of Authenticity," Vikram Chandra, author of *Red Earth and Pouring Rain* writes:

> I noticed the constant hum of this rhetoric, this anxiety about the anxiety of Indianness, this notion of a real reality that was being distorted by "Third World cosmopolitans," this fear of an all-devouring and all-distorting West. I heard it in conversations, in critical texts, in reviews. And Indians who wrote in English were one of the prime locations for this rhetoric to test itself, to make its declarations of power and belonging, to announce its possession of certain territories and its right to delineate lines of control.

The final sentence of this passage is especially instructive. Questions of authenticity are about power. Who has the power to define the boundaries of group membership, to define who belongs, to define who is authentic to a particular culture or group? In her TED talk, "The Danger of a Single Story," Chimamanda Ngozi Adichie relates the following story of her time in college:

> A professor ... once told me that my novel was not 'authentically African.' Now, I was quite willing to contend that there were a number of things wrong with the novel, that it had failed in a number of places. But I had not quite imagined that it had failed at achieving something called African authenticity. In fact I did not know what African authenticity was. The professor told me that my characters were too much like him, an educated and middle-class

man. My characters drove cars. They were not starving. Therefore they were not authentically African.

Notions of authenticity are used to police the boundaries of group culture, from both within and outside of groups.

Even as we critique the use of notions of authenticity to police groups of people, this does not simply leave us to an "anything goes" relativism. Who speaks matters. So does it matter how a group is represented and by whom. We must question our insider and outsider status within groups we represent, knowing that it is never one or the other. As Patricia Hill Collins reminds us, often we are "outsiders within." Writers from dominant groups must interrogate the representations they produce about groups to which they do not belong. By the same turn, the demand that one represent a group to which one belongs must be interrogated as well. It is just as problematic to expect people from marginalized groups to be perfectly self-knowing. Marginalized folks are caught within the colonial discourse as well. The task lies in holding the tensions, contradictions, and quandaries as we write within the politics of authenticity.

Author

Historically, different meanings have been attributed to the term "author," or related terms "poet" and "writer." From Longinus's "great soul" to Shelley's famous claim that poets are "the unacknowledged legislators of the world" to Emerson's conception of the poet as "the true and only doctor," we see a range of ways of characterizing the poet, writer, or author.

In a book devoted to defining the term "author," Andrew Bennett recounts a history of authorship found in the term's etymology: Bennett notes that *The Oxford English Dictionary* records that the word "author" comes from the Latin verb *augere*, "to make, to grow, originate, promote, increase," which developed into the words *auctor* and *auctoritas* in the medieval period. The notion of the author as "someone who 'originates or gives existence to anything'" appeared in Chaucer's time with the words *auctor*, *auctour*, and later *aucthour* and *author*. Later, in the eighteenth century, a number of words entered the language (e.g., "authorial," "authoring," "authorism," "authorless," "authorling," "authorly," and "authorship") that demonstrate an increasing interest in the role of the author.

The "author" and the "poet" become special personae in the cultural imaginary. In the Western aesthetic tradition, the poet has sometimes been characterized in spiritual terms. Poets have been conceived as "liberating gods," as Emerson uses the term in "The Poet"—or as holders of a "sacred office," as Henry James is known for saying. As early as the writings of Homer, Monroe Beardsley notes, "the functions of poet and seer, or prophet, were already distinguished," yet in ancient Greece these two figures were at times linked: "For both the poet and the seer, like the oracle, spoke in heightened language, in words that moved and dazzled, with an inexplicable magic power" (Beardsley 25).

The poet is sometimes conceived as someone who has a greater capacity to feel than other people, although the nature of the poet's emotion is not different from that of others (i.e., in Wordsworth's words, the poet traffics in the "general passions and thoughts and feelings of men" and is "nothing differing in kind from other men, but only in degree"(8)).The poet is, in Wordsworth's view, "endowed with more lively sensibility, more enthusiasm and tenderness" and he (Wordsworth uses the male pronoun) "has a greater knowledge of human nature, and a more comprehensive soul, than are supposed to be common upon mankind." The poet is "affected more than other men by absent things as if they were present" (8). For P.B. Shelley, the poet is "more delicately organized than other men, and sensible to pain and pleasure, both his own and that of others, in a degree unknown to them" (612). The poet's capacities make him most acutely human: "In the intervals of inspiration," Shelley writes, "a poet becomes a man" (612).

These descriptions represent an essentializing tendency in discussions of authorship—as they construct an image of the poet, telling us what and who a poet must be. In setting these descriptors, these aesthetic thinkers reinforce a particular set of identities as belonging to the status of poet. Who gets to decide who possesses the definitive qualities of the poet or author? Who decides how a person will be judged in relation to cultural ideas of author? The terms set by the authors listed above were set by men—men who had access to certain forms of social capital. The men listed above lived in countries that were seats of colonial power at the time of their writing.

The word "author" is tied to the word "authority." To have the status of an author is to have a status of authority. In Gail Stygall's terms, from her essay "Resisting Privilege," there is a set of rights and licenses that comes with the identity of the "author": among these is "the right to transgress conventions" (324). The *author*'s break in conventions is considered to be artful, whereas the *novice*'s break in convention may be read as an error. For example, imagine a text that makes ample use of parataxis. Someone who has the status of "author" or "poet" may be understood to be using parataxis purposefully, while the same text may be judged as poorly constructed if its writer is not given the status of "author" or "poet." The fragments in this text may be considered to be important formal choices if the writer is called "poet," when those same fragments might be called grammatical errors and failures in reasoning if the writer is not granted the status of "author" or "poet."

In addition to the right to transgress conventions, Norma Klahn writes in an essay titled "Literary (Re)Mappings" of another right that comes with authorship: the status of the author enables one to have a say in one's own history. Speaking of Chicana feminist autobiographers, Klahn notes how "these writers gained authority and inserted themselves into a history that had excluded them, their people, culture, and language" through claiming the identity of author for themselves (118).

It is not always easy to claim the identity of an author. The ease with which one can claim the identity has much to do with the social hierarchies we find in our cultures. Think about who gets to play the part of the author in Blockbuster films such as *Dead Poets Society* (1989), *Wonder Boys* (2000), *Finding Forrester* (2000), *Adaptation* (2002), *Midnight in Paris* (2011), *Ruby Sparks* (2012), *The Words* (2012), and *Perks of Being a Wallflower* (2012). More often than not, we see a white, male, able-bodied actor playing the part of the author. This small sampling of writer films points to the exclusions of certain identities from the title of author.

Given this context, the significance of identifying oneself with the word "author" means something different to different people. Klahn writes of how publishing as an author means something particular for those who are "in a culture where a *mujer que publica* is admonished as *una mujer pública*, a wicked woman who contests the positions sanctioned by a still male-dominated society" (126). Understanding these complexities, and the politics of the author-identity, is important work for the creative writer. We can reflect: Who are we most likely to call an "author"? How do we use the idea of an author? And who is served by our use of the term?

Layered into these complex questions is the additional question of whether a text is "authored" at all. Our existing definitions of "author" make a number of assumptions about textual production that have been called into question by theorists such as Michel Foucault, Roland Barthes, and Jacques Derrida. Specifically, these theorists have questioned the common idea that a single, unitary person called "author" produces a text in "sovereign solitude," to use Derrida's term. These theorists show that while notions of the "author" serve to help us organize the texts we encounter, the author is ultimately a function of the text—rather than the text being a manifestation of an author. The author becomes a cultural image that readers superimpose on future texts. As Foucault explains, when we try to preserve the author we are imposing an "ideological figure by which one marks the manner in which we fear the proliferation of meaning" (Foucault, in Finkelstein and McCleary 230). In other words, the "author," as a construct, teaches us to be interested in "expression" and "the insertion of a subject into language," to use Foucault's terms (Foucault in Adams and Searle 139). But Foucault and Barthes, in different ways, posit that "writing is not restricted to the confines of interiority" (139). Foucault is interested in studying "the modifications and variations, within any culture, of modes of circulation, valorization, attribution, and appropriation," and these interests coincide with the ways in which "discourse is articulated on the basis of social relationships" (147).

We know that readers are often interested in an author's personality. Readers may become fans and admirers of the people they imagine J.K. Rowling or Toni Morrison to be. This readerly interest in the author's personality developed in the nineteenth and twentieth centuries to focus on the unique attributes or unique "personality" of the person behind the text. But the texts we read are not fully governed by that personality. Indeed, the meaning that we derive at in our reading practices is meaning that we "make" or co-create, based on our knowledge of innumerable interlacing codes and texts and cultural ideas. Barthes's famous essay "The Death of the Author" articulates how every text is an impersonal, open sea of signification. The absence or death of the author replaces the idea of "literary genius" with an activity of writing and reading that cannot be grounded in any pre-given subject-position. So, authors are not owners and controllers of all they say. Authors are a composite of discourses. And the reading of every text is always beyond the author's control. Every piece of writing is shaped by its imbrication in social forces, its genre and context, and its being taken up by the meaning-making strategies of the reader within a constellation of cultural forces.

We can see the blurring of the identities of reader and writer perhaps most clearly in examples of fan-fiction where the reader offers a reading of a book by writing or rewriting it. Technologies that allow for the production and distribution of fan-fiction enable authorship to become a generalized practice. A *Seed* magazine article famously claimed that we are on the verge of "nearly universal authorship"—with nearly everyone publishing work available to at least 100 people.

Barthes and Foucault help us to destabilize an idea of the author as an autonomous owner of, and free authority on, their words. But we should also preserve a space for what the claim to an authorial identity can mean for some writers, particularly those who have historically been excluded from cultural images of the author. Claiming authorial authority may be an important political gesture for a writer who also acknowledges her texts's connectedness to what is beyond her control. Her texts are tied to a web of meaning that composes her and that she composes within. She may reject the idea of a single author-self, and she may write within community—where each person or being holds a part of the story. She may, even still, claim a sense of "authorship," amid both the limits and possibilities of this term. "Authorship" is tied to exclusionary histories that fantasize a notion of a sovereign genius and originator of a text. However, for the person who these histories of authorship have excluded, there may be power in writing oneself into the notions of sovereignty and authority that have been tied to the construct we call "author." It might be said that the author, as a construct, was declared "dead" by white men before many had a chance to live it. When we speak of the "author," then, we should do so with awareness of how we locate ourselves differently in relation to it, and to its histories.

Belonging

In the poem "Belonging," Alla Renée Bozarth writes that home "becomes different places" and makes one "feel alive, /important and safe" (Bozarth 1995). The poem speaks to the themes of place, recognition, and change which are sutured to the notion of belonging. Belonging is about being connected to something larger than oneself: "You have stars/in your bones" and "You belong to the land," the poem continues. Ultimately the notion of belonging raises questions central to our ideas about personhood, community, place, and power. There are many dimensions to the notion of belonging: social, political, and affective.

In the discipline of psychology, Maslow (1943) suggested that belonging is a fundamental human need. He characterized "belongingness," or the need to be accepted within a group, as one of five human needs in his "hierarchy of needs," along with physical/ bodily needs, safety, self-esteem, and self-actualization. Maslow's hierarchy treats belonging as an essential characteristic of human beings.

Critical theorists have deployed a more nuanced conceptualization of belonging, showing how belonging is linked to power relations.

Nira Yuval-Davis distinguishes between belonging and the politics of belonging, writing:

> Belonging is about emotional attachment, about feeling 'at home' and, as Michael Ignatieff points out, about feeling 'safe' ... Belonging tends to be naturalized, and becomes articulated and politicized only when it is threatened in some way. The politics of belonging comprises specific political projects aimed at constructing belonging in particular ways to particular collectivities that are, at the same time, themselves being constructed by these projects in very particular ways. (Yuval-Davis 2006, 197)

Students of creative writing can usefully take up questions of belonging in ways which represent people in all the diverse ways they are situated within, outside, and between various communities. Belonging may be a key theme or motif in our literary work. The question of belonging also shapes our work beyond the page, in our interactions with each other in workshop, and in the classroom. The notion of belonging is embedded in messages about who "belongs" to the identity-categories of poet, writer, author. The notion of belonging may be hidden behind some of what we say when we evaluate a work of literature—as many evaluations have behind them premises about what "belongs" within the sphere we call literature. Questions of belonging are political questions. Our notions of belonging, however implicit and hidden they may be, have the potential to either calcify or dislodge the status quo.

The forms of inequity and oppression that are elsewhere cited in this book are related to belonging. Political belonging opens out onto questions of nationhood, citizenship, borders, and the State. In *Who*

Sings the Nation-State?: Language, Politics, Belonging, Judith Butler links belonging to the state and citizenship. She writes:

> We might expect that the state presupposes modes of juridical belonging, at least minimally, but since the state can be precisely what expels and suspends modes of legal protection and obligation, the state can put us, some of us, in quite a state. It can signify the source of non belonging, even produce that nonbelonging as a quasi-permanent state. (Butler and Spivak 2010, 3–4)

In the same essay, Butler highlights the role of the State in juridical belonging and the conditions which "govern how and where we may move, associate, work, and speak" (4). Questions of belonging are often questions of state power—a relation that becomes obvious when we consider incarceration: which is, Tiffany Willoughby-Herard notes, "one of the most severe and excessive forms of teaching people that their primary relationship of belonging is to the state as its property."

Questions of national belonging have been particularly pervasive in Black British Cultural Studies. Stuart Hall and Paul Gilroy, for example, demonstrate the ways in which Britishness is sutured to whiteness, foreclosing the possibilities of social and political belonging for formerly colonized subjects migrating to the metropole (Hall 1993; Gilroy 1993). The centrality of "feeling at home" connects the notion of belonging to the concepts of diaspora, nation, and Other, also included in this text.

Recognition is also central to belonging; it is the basis on which belonging is founded and has implications for our political horizons. To whom is a recognition claim made? Often, it is the State, itself a frequent purveyor of violence and exclusion. The implications of this for political struggle are important to unpack.

Nancy Fraser (2000) problematizes recognition as the basis for political claims-making. In her *New Left Review* article, "Rethinking Recognition," she contrasts recognition claims with claims for material redistribution. Lamenting how a politics of recognition can obfuscate and hinder material change, Fraser finds the politics of recognition to be "disturbing on two counts":

> First, this move from redistribution to recognition is occurring despite—or because of—an acceleration of economic globalization, at a time when an aggressively expanding capitalism is radically exacerbating economic inequality. In this context, questions of recognition are serving less to supplement, complicate and enrich redistributive struggles than to marginalize, eclipse and displace them. I shall call this *the problem of displacement.* Second, today's recognition struggles are occurring at a moment of hugely increasing transcultural interaction and communication, when accelerated migration and global media flows are hybridizing and pluralizing cultural forms. Yet the routes such struggles take often serve not to promote respectful interaction within increasingly multicultural contexts, but to drastically simplify and reify group identities. They tend, rather, to encourage separatism, intolerance and chauvinism, patriarchalism and authoritarianism. I shall call this *the problem of reification.* (108)

Extending this point, Elizabeth Povinelli (2011) argues that legitimation crises have provoked the adoption of "formal or informal policies of cultural recognition (or cognate policies such as multiculturalism) as a strategy for addressing the challenge of internal and external difference" (25). Such forms of recognition risk forced assimilation, co-optation, and political neutering.

Nancy Fraser and Elizabeth Povinelli demonstrate the limits of the politics of recognition, and they expose some of what is at stake in the politics of belonging. Belonging is an important consideration in terms of conceptualizing the relationship of people to their environment. Bell hooks connects belonging to a notion of place, as well as a sense of direction and meaningfulness in life—the question *where* am I going? So often, in exploring what it means to belong, we ask: *where* do I belong? In *Belonging: A Culture of Place*, hooks writes:

> Like many of my contemporaries I have yearned to find my place in this world, to have a sense of homecoming, a sense of being wedded to a place. Searching for a place to belong I make a list of what I will need to create firm ground. At the top of the list I write: 'I need to live where I can walk. I need to be able to walk to work, to the store, to a place where I can sit and drink tea and fellowship. Walking, I will establish my presence, as one who is claiming the earth, creating a sense of belonging, a culture of place.' (2)

Belonging is fastened to place, environment, and land. These are themes ripe for exploration in creative writing. Given histories of conquest, enslavement, and violence, these are also questions of intersecting forms of power and privilege.

Body

The body, the physical form of a human or other living being, has been a preoccupation for thinkers and writers for centuries; however, it is only recently that critical scholars have made the body and the concept of embodiment central to our frames for understanding power and the social. When writing identity, creative writers think through the ways that bodies enter and are figured in their texts.

In modern Western societies, the body/mind dichotomy has been bound up with power relations. As Eva Cherniavsky (2007) writes,

> For Christian theology as for speculative philosophy in the West, the body figures as the devalued term in a structuring dualism of body/soul (in sacred thought) and body/mind (in secular traditions). These dualisms apprehend the body as a material substrate of human life that is fundamentally distinct from and subordinated to the privileged term in the dichotomy (mind, soul), which alone comprehends the human capacity for knowledge and self-knowledge, as well as the repertoire of human sensibilities, dispositions, and affects on which the salvation, expression, or advancement of humanity is understood to depend. (26)

Western thought has been structured by binaries: feminine/masculine, black/white, nature/culture, and body/mind. In the above passage, Cherniavsky points to how positive meanings have tended to attach to one side of the binary, while the other side is "devalued." Some bodies are marked as different and deviant while others are marked as normal. This has profound implications for marginalized populations.

A binary between body/mind is powerful. As Susan Bordo (1995) contends, the body/mind split, often referred to as Cartesian Dualism, has been "deployed and socially embodied in medicine, law, literary and artistic representations" (13). Women, people of color, and disabled folks have often been confined to the realm of the body. For example, the capacity of some people to bear children is often used to identify those people more closely with bodies and thus reduce estimation of the capacities of the mind. People of color have been overidentified with and through bodily features. An example of this is the persistent use of animalistic imagery in representations of people of color. Stereotypes persistently link Black people to animals and physical prowess, rather than intellectual capacities. These ideas impact people in real, material ways, and in lived experience.

Given that aesthetics has historically been conceived as distinctly sensorial practice—with the understanding that art works upon the senses and creates sensations for the body—writers have a germane medium to interrogate binary thinking.

In refusing a simple dichotomy between body and mind, we can denaturalize dualistic approaches to the body. We can conceive of the body as a social text, as Stuart Hall does in his elucidation of race as "a floating signifier." The body as social text is also decoded in Judith

Butler's theory of gender performativity. (See the entries for race and gender in this text for further discussion of this point.) In approaches such as those of Stuart Hall and Judith Butler, "the body" is taken up in the mobilization of power and there is no body prior to the social meanings which bring it into being. Butler (1988), for example, rejects a naturalized idea of the body completely. She argues that the sexed body is *an effect* of gender, rather than something that precedes it. We perform gender through "a stylized repetition of acts," bodily acts (519). This produces a gendered identity, but also produces the notion of sex.

In making this argument, Butler relies on a phenomenological approach to the body. A philosophical movement concerned with experience and consciousness, rather than essences, phenomenology was founded by Edmund Husserl in the early years of the twentieth century. As Butler neatly summarizes, "the phenomenological theory of 'acts', espoused by Edmund Husserl and Maurice Merleau-Ponty, among others, seeks to explain the mundane way in which social agents constitute social reality through language, gesture, and all manner of symbolic social sign" (519).

In this vein, Maurice Merleau-Ponty maintained that the body is an historical idea, as well as a set of possibilities to be continually realized. In making these claims, Merleau-Ponty means that the body gains its meaning through its concrete and historically mediated expression in the world. The body's manifestation in the world is not predetermined by a fixed essence; it emerges within specific configurations of historical possibility which are open to contestation and change. Gilles Deleuze frames the problem of the body in terms that illuminate this concept. In writing about Spinoza, Deleuze (1992) asks: "What Can a Body Do?" Here Deleuze focuses on capabilities and possibilities, rather than essences or ideals.

These notions of capability and possibility pose rich and complex questions. Judith Butler reflects on the question "what can a body do?" in the film "Examined Life," as she takes a walk with disability rights activist Sunaura Taylor:

> We usually ask, 'what is a body' or 'what is the ideal form of a body' or, you know, what is the difference between the body and the soul and that kind of thing. But 'what can a body do' is a different question. It isolates a set of capacities, and a set of instrumentalities or actions, and we are kind of assemblages of those things and I like this idea. It's not like there's an essence and it's not that there's an ideal morphology, you know, what a body should look like. It's exactly not that question. Or what a body should move like. And one of the things that I have found in thinking about gender and even violence against sexual minorities or gender minorities (people whose gender presentation doesn't conform with standard ideals of femininity or masculinity) is that very often it comes down to, you know, how people walk, how they use their hips, what they do with their body parts.

As this excerpt from the film demonstrates, we have to understand the cultural meanings of the body and the constructedness of the body in order to unpack the material violence faced by marginalized people.

Celebrated writer, Ta-Nehisi Coates (2015) provides a compelling meditation on the body and race in his work. He argues that "in America, it is traditional to destroy the black body—*it is heritage*" (103). In order to write the intricacies of antiblackness, we have to understand the way that it reaches the body. There is a relationship between symbolic violence and material force. Throughout the book *Between the World and Me*, Coates notes the sacredness and vulnerability of the body. He writes, "When they shatter the body they shatter everything" (113). Echoing W.E.B. Du Bois and Frantz Fanon before him, Coates articulates the disembodiment of antiblackness as a kind of terrorism or world-shattering force. He uses "disembodiment" as a one-word refrain, demonstrating how the threat and presence of different types of disembodiment are the "demon that pushed middle-class black survivors into aggressive passivity, our conversation restrained in public quarters, our best manners on display, our hands never out of pockets, our whole manner ordered as if to say 'I make no sudden moves.'" Disembodiment is "the serpent of school years, demanding I be twice as good, though I was but a boy" (114).

The body is central to systems of oppression. The experience of oppression is an embodied experience. From the persistent disregard for Black pain in medical settings (Holpuch 2016) and the life-shortening impacts of racialized stress (AAPF 2018) to the policing of manners and mundane bodily acts, the relationship between oppression, privilege, and the body is central to how we write identity and intersectional lives.

How can we move into a different relationship to bodies and their vulnerability? A wide variety of activist work takes up these questions in what has been termed healing justice. This has been a central aspect of the Movement for Black Lives in the early years of the twenty-first century. Defining the orientation to social justice, Cara Page from the Kindred Southern Healing Justice Collective explains, "healing justice ... identifies how we can holistically respond to and intervene in generational trauma and violence, and to bring collective practices that can impact and transform the consequences of oppression on our bodies, hearts and minds" (qtd. in Hemphill). Healing justice is about attending to our full selves as we engage in social transformation, recognizing the incredible toll that these systems and activist work take on our bodies, minds, and spirits. Roxana Ng, as another example, elaborates an embodied pedagogy in terms of interconnectedness between spirit-mind-body.

If you are reading this, you currently have a body. This is something we all share. However, our experience of embodiment is vast and differentiated. Some of us have thin bodies or tall bodies; others of us have bodies in pain. Our experience of embodiment is also bound up with power relations and the social meanings projected onto our bodies. In this sense, our bodies are not entirely our own. We cannot control the meanings attached to our bodies in social settings any more than we can control the likelihood that we will grow older and die. These are themes of great significance for creative writers.

Class

Like gender and race, the keyword "class" holds a space of central importance in intersectionality, and it is a key concept to consider in the creative writing workshop. At a basic level, class refers to a status or rank in society. Joan Acker (2006) defines class "as differing and unequal situations in access to and control over the means of provisioning and survival" (55). Today, class most often names the ways in which people's access to basic needs is mediated in a capitalist economy by the relations of wage labor, control over the means of production, and the exploitation which makes profit possible.

Any intellectual history of the concept of class counts the work of Karl Marx as formative, if not foundational. Marx, publishing the first of three volumes of *Capital* in 1867, investigated the workings of a distinctively capitalist mode of production. This mode of production was distinctively capitalist for many reasons, including a distinctive form of private property. Marx highlights the fluid and mobile nature of capital, which sometimes appeared in the form of money, but also appeared as other aspects of production such as machinery, land, and materials. Workers are coerced into the labor market, having no choice but to sell their capacity to labor for the means of subsistence.

Marx theorized these workers, the Proletariat, as the great force of history, destined to overthrow the capitalist system, evolving toward a communist system.

Importantly, Marx theorized class in the context of Europe and, in many ways, failed to see the ways that colonialism was central to the operation of capital from a global perspective. Postcolonial theorists have shown how a Eurocentric notion of class and class consciousness could not be simply applied to conditions outside of Europe. However, the concept of class has continued to be an important keyword for understanding economic and social relations into the twenty-first century.

Class is a powerful force in national life, even as a nation's collective narratives often portray a classless society where one's success is based on merit. In the United States, collective narratives are often characterized by an idea that the economic circumstances of one's birth do not fix one's position in society and that there is boundless opportunity to improve one's situation in life. Howard Zinn writes of this myth and its presence in US discourse in saying,

> I've always resented the smug statements of politicians, media commentators, corporate executives who talked of how, in America, if you worked hard you would become rich. The meaning of that was if you were poor it was because you hadn't worked hard enough. I knew this was a lie, about my father and millions of others, men and women who worked harder than anyone, harder than financiers and politicians.

Zinn's statement shows how the American "bootstraps" myth (i.e., the myth that if you work hard you can "pull yourself up by your bootstraps" and find upward mobility) is damaging.

To understand this harmful myth, we have to look beyond income and also examine differences in wealth. While income, the "amount of money brought into a household in one year," is incredibly important, it provides an incomplete picture of the resources at one's disposal (Andersen and Collins 61). Imagine two college seniors at graduation: Catherine and Alicia. They both have found paid internships for their first year out of college, paying $25K. This internship is, for each person, their sole source of income. However, Catherine's parents gift her a car at graduation and allow her to live in a condo they own in the city. Alicia has substantial student loans, while Catherine's parents paid for college. If we only look to their income, their situations look similar. When we broaden our view to encompass wealth, we see something very different about their class situations. Wealth encompasses all of one's financial assets, subtracting one's debt. Income is one part of wealth, but it also includes things like property. Wealth is significant in determining one's class position in society. Wealth is also cumulative; wealth is passed down from generation to generation. It's important to remember that within histories of colonialism, enslavement, and other forms of oppression, some have been enabled to accumulate wealth at the expense of others.

Class, "a system that differentially structures group access to economic, political, cultural and social resources," shapes life chances. Research shows that class impacts health outcomes, the likelihood of exposure to environmental toxins, educational attainment, and myriad other facets of life. Class is also about issues of comportment and social capital: As Bennett et al. (2013) explain, "Elitism, privilege, hereditary advantage, and snobbery have been constant focal points of social conflict and mobilization ... The idea of class distinction persists in a variety of social evaluations of people and things—being classy, having class, distinctions between different classes of travelers in planes, boats, and trains, and so on" (39). In discussions of literature, this shows up in distinctions between "high" and "low" art, which is often cloaked in other terms (e.g., "literary" versus "genre" fiction). Class provides a means of thinking critically about how these "distinctions," to use Bourdieu's term, are erected and maintained.

But there are limitations to many analyses of class. Traditional Marxist explanations of class have tended to focus on white, male workers. If we look at the experiences of white working-class women, and men and women of color, we see some different things about how class operates in social life.

Feminist scholars such as Joan Acker (2006) have emphasized the need to expand notions of "the economy," beyond conventional notions of the economic limited to "the production of goods and services, of material and nonmaterial things, their exchange for money in markets, and the distribution of the surplus from that exchange" (53). Acker notes how "paid employment in production of goods and services for markets has defined 'work' and 'class'" (53). She argues for paying attention to reproductive and unpaid labor in order to understand how class is racialized and gendered.

Race and class are fundamentally bound up with one another. In *Where We Stand: Class Matters*, bell hooks (2000) also explores their connections:

Black folks with money think about class more than most people do in this society. They know that most of the white people around them believe all black people are poor, even the ones with fancy suits and tailored shirts wearing Rolex watches and carrying leather briefcases. Poverty in the white mind is always primarily black. Even though the white poor are many, living in suburbs and rural areas, they remain invisible. The black poor are everywhere, or so many white people think. (4)

Cedric Robinson uses the conceptual vocabulary of racial capitalism to understand the complex relationship between race and class in the United States. Robinson's work has been influential. In the introduction to the *Boston Review*'s issue on Race, Capitalism and Justice, Robin D.G. Kelley writes of Robinson's concept:

Robinson challenged the Marxist idea that capitalism was a revolutionary negation of feudalism. Instead capitalism emerged within the feudal order and flowered in the cultural soil of a Western civilization already thoroughly infused with racialism. Capitalism and racism, in other words, did not break from the old order but rather evolved from it to produce a modern world system of "racial capitalism" dependent on slavery, violence, imperialism, and genocide. Capitalism was "racial" not because of some conspiracy to divide workers or justify slavery and dispossession, but because racialism had already permeated Western feudal society. The first European proletarians were *racial* subjects (Irish, Jews, Roma or Gypsies, Slavs, etc.) and they were victims of dispossession (enclosure), colonialism, and slavery *within Europe*. Indeed, Robinson suggested that racialization within Europe was very much a *colonial* process involving invasion, settlement, expropriation, and racial hierarchy. (7)

Class is racialized, and racialized groups are stratified by class. Intersectionality asks creative writers to develop a more nuanced reading of the imbrication of multiple systems of difference in our work. Notions of art, craft, and writing are often underwritten with classism. In the words of Alison Stine:

> Art is not the class I was born into. It's not only that writing doesn't pay well; it costs a lot of money for the privilege of not being paid, even for the *consideration* of not being paid. It's not simply that paying magazines' submission fees is a luxury for me and for many others, but that being an unpaid intern—a funnel toward publication or an editorial position—is a pipedream when you're juggling which of the bills to pay this month, wondering if water is more important than heat.

Colonialism

Colonialism refers to "the extension of a nation's sovereignty over territory and people both within and outside its own boundaries, as well as the beliefs used to legitimate this domination" (Bosworth and Flavin 2). Colonialism has a material dimension of economic and political domination through institutions, as well as an ideological dimension, through the construction of cultural ideas and practices which naturalize the material dimensions.

The terms "colonialism" and "imperialism" are often used interchangeably. In *Culture and Imperialism*, Edward Said (1994) offers the following distinction, which is instructive: "'imperialism' means the practice, the theory, and the attitudes of a dominating metropolitan centre ruling a distant territory; 'colonialism', which is almost always a consequence of imperialism, is the implanting of settlements on distant territory" (9).

Modern colonialism is fundamentally bound up with the development of a capitalist mode of production. Capitalism requires expansion into new markets, and colonial territories provided natural resources, labor, and agricultural commodities which funded Western wealth and consumption. As the title of Walter Rodney's famous book suggests, "Europe Underdeveloped Africa." The wealth and power of many European countries and the United States are built on colonialism, enslavement, and exploitation.

While material exploitation often seems most urgent, colonial domination's cultural components are particularly important for creative writers to understand. As Said writes:

> Neither imperialism, nor colonialism is a simple act of accumulation and acquisition. Both are supported and perhaps even impelled by impressive ideological formations that include notions that certain territories and people require and beseech domination, as well as forms of knowledge affiliated with domination: the vocabulary of classic nineteenth-century imperial culture is plentiful with words and concepts like "inferior" or "subject races," "subordinate peoples," "dependency," "expansion," and "authority." Out of the imperial experiences, notions about culture were clarified, reinforced, criticized, or rejected.

European colonialism was in part justified through literary ideas about cultural superiority. For example, Rudyard Kipling's 1899 poem "The White Man's Burden … " is a classic example of the power of literature to justify domination. The poem encouraged the United States to colonize the Philippine Islands. The poem begins

> Take up the White Man's burden
> Send forth the best ye breed
> Go bind your sons to exile
> To serve your captives' need;

To wait in heavy harness,

On fluttered folk and wild

Your new-caught, sullen peoples,

Half-devil and half-child.

Figuring the Filipino people as "half-devil and half-child" laid the groundwork for American Empire and the idea that subjugation of these islands was a noble enterprise.

Our modern world has been profoundly shaped by Western imperialism and European colonization. Notions of race, gender, class, and sexuality have all been influenced by these forces, both historically and in the present. Aimé Césaire wrote in *Discourse on Colonialism* (1950) that "Colonization = thing-ification" (42). In other words, under colonialism the colonized is objectified, turned into a "thing" that is at the colonizing power's disposal. Césaire was one of the founders of the Négritude movement, writing at a time when many colonized countries were winning their fights for independence. Robin D.G. Kelley (1999) writes of this age of decolonization in Africa, Asia, and Latin America: "The old empires were on the verge of collapse, thanks in part to a world war against fascism that left Europe in material, spiritual, and philosophical shambles." Césaire's literary writing worked to show how colonialism depended on ideologies that sought to dehumanize the colonized and render the native an object, an Other. Kelley lists some of the critical contributions of *Discourse on Colonialism*:

First, its recasting of the history of Western Civilization helps us locate the origins of fascism within colonialism itself; hence, within the very traditions of humanism, critics believed fascism threatened. Second, Césaire was neither confused about Marxism nor masquerading as a Marxist when he wrote *Discourse*. On the contrary, he was attempting to revise Marx, along the lines of his predecessors such as W.E.B. Du Bois and M.N. Roy, by suggesting that the anticolonial struggle supersedes the proletarian revolution as the fundamental historical movement of the period. The implications are enormous: the coming revolution was not posed in terms of capitalism versus socialism ... , but in terms of the complete and total overthrow of a racist, colonialist system that would open the way to imagine a whole new world.

Césaire's work presaged the later development of postcolonial theory and a radical questioning of the terms of Marxist thought.

An intersectional framework is necessary to fully unpack colonial discourse. As scholars have built on Césaire's work and examined the wide varieties of colonial violence throughout the world, they have shown how race, gender, sexuality, and other logics of domination were central to European colonial enterprises. Andrea Smith (2005) argues that sexual violence is a central tool of colonialism. Colonialism was central to the development of "race." Indeed, as Ann Laura Stoler (2006) identifies, race is "a central colonial sorting technique" (2). Stoler elucidates this point in "Intimidations of Empire: Predicaments of the Tactile and Unseen":

Racial thinking secures racial designations in a language of biology and fixity and in the quest for a visual set of physical differences to index that which is not "self-evident" or visible—neither easy to agree on nor easy to see. Scientific taxonomies of race stress the "concrete" measures of racial membership, but they, like social taxonomies, depend implicitly on a belief in the different sensibilities and sensory regimes imagined to distinguish human kinds. Within these racial grammars distinct affective capacities get assigned to specific populations. This comparative imagining does not necessarily ascribe a different repertoire of sentiments to different groups. Rather certain groups are imagined to have more limited emotive capacities or are endowed with more intense displays of affective expression. (2)

Here Stoler begins to show us how racial hierarchies and colonial encounters relied on notions of affect. Stoler, along with Lisa Lowe and others, investigates colonialism with an eye toward racialized and gendered notions of affect and what they call *domains of the intimate* or *intimacies*. Stoler writes,

Colonial authority depended on shaping appropriate and reasoned affect (where one's sympathies should lie), severing some intimate bonds and establishing others (which offspring would be acknowledged as one's own) establishing what constituted moral sentiments (family honor or patriotic duty); in short, colonial authority rested on educating the proper distribution of sentiments and desires.

What this shows us is the far-reaching work of colonial enterprises. Human beings do not naturally "stay in their places," so colonialism required that the most intimate aspects of life had to be detailed and managed. Otherwise, humans tend to cross boundaries, forming friendships, sexual relationships, and trust with those toward whom they are supposed to feel superior. As they attempted to envelope the full sphere of human experience within their regimes, colonial enterprises show us the necessity of an intersectional framework which demonstrates how race, gender, sexuality, and other axes of difference buttress one another and are never fully separable. It is readily apparent how colonialism has worked upon the full range of human experience and human identity.

Take sexuality, for example. Robert Young (1995) deploys the term "colonial desire" to name the ways in which colonial discourse was suffused with sexuality. Lisa Lowe argues that "the colonial management of sexuality, affect, marriage, and family among the colonized formed a central part of the microphysics of colonial rule" (195). Her use of the term microphysics here is important. While colonialism has been studied from the scale of large world processes, these postcolonial feminist thinkers show that the micro-level, down to the intimacies of the household and bedroom, "are not microcosms of empire but its marrow" (Stoler 3).

It is important to understand the great varieties of colonial experience. Indigenous intellectuals have differentiated between neo-colonialism, where a people have won independence but nonetheless remain subjugated by colonial powers both materially and culturally; metropole colonialism, with reference to the Greek *metropolis* meaning "mother city" (the UK is a classic example of this variety, where the seat of colony power is at a distance in a homeland, while resources are extracted from distant colonies); and settler colonialism, where settlers come to permanently occupy and control Indigenous lands. Settler colonialism rests on the attempted elimination of Indigenous resistance and often Indigenous peoples themselves. Often assertions of settler sovereignty are coupled with narratives of settler belonging, such that settlers co-opt the cultural practices of the colonized.

Coloniality is a dynamic of the creative writing workshop. As Chimamanda Ngozi Adichie argues in "The Danger of a Single Story,"

There is a word, an Igbo word, that I think about whenever I think about the power structures of the world, and it is "nkali." It's a noun that loosely translates to "to be greater than another." Like our economic and political worlds, stories too are defined by the principle of nkali. How they are told, who tells them, when they're told, how many stories are told, are really dependent on power. Power is the ability not just to tell the story of another person, but to make it the definitive story of that person.

Critical creative writers must reflect upon how they will interact with the colonial histories and colonial presents of the land on which they, their characters, and their audiences live.

Community

Etymology: < Anglo-Norman and Middle French *communité, comunité* joint ownership (*c*1130 in Old French; also in Old French as *communeté*), relations, association (*c*1150 or earlier in Anglo-Norman), nation or state (12th cent.), body of people who live in the same place, usually sharing a common cultural or ethnic identity (*c*1370), religious society (1378) < classical Latin *commūnitāt-, commūnitās* joint possession or use, participation, sharing, social relationship, fellowship, organized society, shared nature or quality, kinship, obligingness, in post-classical Latin also right of common, body of people living in a town (frequently from 12th cent. in British sources), common people, religious society, monastic body (from 13th cent. in British sources)

The *Oxford English Dictionary* provides the above passage for the etymology of the use of "community" in the English language. Used to name a group of people sharing in a social relationship, community has a variety of meanings clustered around it, including tones of belonging, sharing, sameness, and solidarity. This term is ubiquitous across the political spectrum, being marshaled for causes as disparate as faith-based marriage-promotion initiatives and the combating of environmental racism.

Community is a powerful valence issue and rhetorical device which should be deployed critically. While generally associated with positive attributes, community is a signifier often underwritten by exclusionary dimensions. Marshaling community as an actor or cause often creates an "us" founded on the exclusion of a "them." These moves are rarely transparent. For writers, it is imperative that we unpack the notions of "us" and "them" which we construct and reproduce in our writing of "community."

We need to ask who is being centered in a given use of "community"? Notions of community have tended to center those who are most powerful in a group. Women of color feminists have pointed this out in relation to articulations of "the Black community" with book titles like "All the women are white, all the men are black, but some of us are brave" appearing in the late 1970s and 1980s. This edited volume, by Gloria Hull, Patricia Bell Scott, and Barbara Smith, articulated the problematic deployment of community in feminist and racial justice movements of the time.

Scholars concerned with political community, the State, and nationalism have also launched vigorous critique of the concept of community. In 1983, Benedict Anderson famously theorized the nation as an "imagined community." Nationalist movements are often undergirded by origin stories characterized by racial purity, patriarchal gender relations, and other exclusionary logics, which are used to legitimate both colonial and postcolonial nationalisms. Geographer Steve Herbert (2005) has conceptualized community as "a trapdoor." Using the example of cut social services in Seattle,

Herbert shows how "community" becomes a rhetorical device with detrimental effects. The State capitalizes on the common notion that community means empowerment. In these rhetorical maneuverings, community becomes a term that is used to off-load responsibilities for which the State once claimed ownership. Loaded up with the responsibility to be self-sustaining and to provide for the sustenance of its members, and stripped of publicly subsidized governmental support, community, Herbert writes, "exists as a false floor, ready to collapse when laden with excessive political expectations." This is one way in which community becomes a "trapdoor." Herbert continues,

> Community functions as a trapdoor in a second sense as well. Part of the ideological advantage of governing through community is the benighted status the term possesses. As noted above, the legitimacy of local self-determination has a long provenance in the United States ... Given the hallowed nature of localized democratic action, projects that foreground community presumably possess great legitimacy. States can thus ostensibly off-load responsibilities to communities with minimal political cost because this can be legitimated as strengthening local control. (853)

But local control is an illusion as communities still exist within State power. Thus, the floor falls out from under the notion of local community-based governance; instead, we find that the constructs of "community" are tools for governing and controlling populations.

Miranda Joseph (2007), following the work of Raymond Williams, further highlights the particular implications of community within a capitalist system, writing,

The discourse of community includes a Romantic narrative that places it prior to 'society,' locating community in a long lost past for which we yearn nostalgically from our current fallen state of alienation, bureaucratization, and rationalization. This discourse also contrasts community with modern capitalist society structurally; the foundation of community is supposed to be social values, while capitalist society is based only on economic value. At the same time, community is often understood to be a problematic remnant of the past, standing in the way of modernization and progress. (58)

Simplistic notions of community, whether considered a haven from capitalism and racism, or a bouy against the polluting effects of modernity, must be questioned. One must ask how is community being deployed and to what effect? How is community deployed in literature? Can we reclaim community?

Consciousness

There are many ways to approach consciousness. The classical liberal tradition treats consciousness as the ideas and attitudes of individuals as they establish the form and texture of social life. In this approach, human beings and their consciousness are conceived of in radically individualistic terms. He (and we use that pronoun deliberately here, as this figure is bound up with Western conceptions of gender and race) is driven by self-interest, and this fundamental orientation determines the shape and content of communities, institutions, and social relations. In this conception of consciousness, Man makes History, and consciousness is not impacted by social relations.

Marxist thinkers have tended to take a very different approach. For Marx, the system of ideas through which people understand their world is dependent on the material circumstances in which those people live. Rather than see consciousness as being radically individualized, intellectuals building on Marx's body of work, as Patricia Ewick and Susan Silbey (1992) note, have tended to understand consciousness as an epiphenomenon, a secondary effect or byproduct, of class (739–740). An individual is "interpellated" into a place within a system by the system's dominant ideology and ideological state apparatuses, to summarize a formulation offered by Louis Althusser. The term "ideological state apparatuses" refers to structures that maintain power subtly, by seeming to secure the internal consent of the people they include; these include political parties, schools, the media, religious institutions, etc. From this perspective, an individual's consciousness is determined by the systems that interpellate them.

The Marxist notion of "false consciousness" exemplifies this approach. Karl Marx did not actually use the term "false consciousness," but rather articulated the concept of ideology, which is bound up with questions of consciousness and power. Georg Lukács introduced the concept of false consciousness into twentieth-century Marxist discourse in *History and Class Consciousness: Studies in Marxist Dialectics*. False consciousness names the way that ideology systemically produces misrepresentations of economic conditions which are internalized by the working classes—i.e., they have a "false consciousness." "False consciousness" refers to the understandings that someone *is in a position to have*, within a given economic order.

Lukács's understanding of false consciousness is taken up to explain why members of the proletariat are not automatically revolutionaries who see the system for what it is and seek to rise up against it. Thus, false consciousness is related to the question: To what degree do people have agency within a given social and economic structure? Antonio Gramsci argued that the working class could indeed influence the terms of consciousness. He articulates a struggle over the dominant representation of the existing social reality. The capitalist class generally exercises hegemony over the terms of ideology, through its control of the instruments of consciousness; but the working class can form its own cultural institutions and exert influence. Gramsci's work (1971) represents a rupture in Marxist conceptions of ideology because it moves us toward a more complex view of working-class consciousness, countering a tendency to view it primarily as the passive tool of the dominant ideology.

Intellectuals approaching consciousness within the frame of cultural practice provide theorization of consciousness that is perhaps more nuanced than either the "Man makes History" or "History makes the Man" conceptualizations. In their elaboration of the concept of "legal consciousness," Ewick and Silbey conceive of consciousness as "a reciprocal process in which the meanings given by individuals to their world ... become repeated, patterned and stabilized, and those institutionalized structures become part of the meaning systems employed by individuals" (741). This process-oriented conception highlights the relational nature of consciousness. The world impacts our conceptual frameworks for apprehending it, and our conceptual schema impacts the world. This approach to consciousness is useful because it centers meaning-making practices and their relationship to material conditions, opening up a more complex dialectic between oppression and resistance. This allows us to represent people in our writing in all of their complex personhood where the "stories people tell about themselves, about their problems, about their society, and about their society's problems are entangled and weave between what's immediately available as a story and what their imaginations are reaching toward" (Gordon 100–101).

Authors of color have theorized consciousness in other terms. For example, W.E.B Du Bois theorized the concept of double consciousness. Du Bois introduced the concept in his famous 1903 volume *The Souls of Black Folks*, which Brent Hayes Edwards calls "the definitive text of the African American literary tradition" (Du Bois vii). Double consciousness names the "peculiar sensation" of being caught between the dominant representations of Black people and one's self. In the following passage—which, Edwards notes, is one of the most often quoted in twentieth-century American literature—Du Bois writes,

> Born with a veil, and gifted with second-sight in this American world,—a world which yields him no true self-consciousness, but only lets him see himself through the revelation of the other world. It is a peculiar sensation, this double-consciousness, this sense of always looking at one's self through the eyes of others, of measuring one's soul by the tape of a world that looks on in amused contempt and pity. One ever feels his two-ness,—an American, a Negro; two souls, two thoughts, two unreconciled strivings; two warring ideals in one dark body, whose dogged strength alone keeps it from being torn asunder. (8)

Du Bois conceives of double consciousness as both a curse and a gift. It both contains a sense of being caught in the gaze of the dominant group and being able to see the nation in a deeper and more complex way.

Gloria Anzaldúa's notion of mestiza consciousness has been transformative as well. Destabilizing notions of racial purity and cultural authenticity, Anzaldúa articulates a hybrid consciousness, *una conciencia de mujer*, a consciousness of the borderlands. This is inseparable from Anzaldúa's identity as a writer:

Writing produces anxiety. Looking inside myself and my experience, looking at my conflicts, engenders anxiety in me. Being a writer feels very much like being a Chicana, or being queer—a lot of squirming, coming up against all sorts of walls. Or its opposite: nothing defined or definite, a boundless, floating state of limbo where I kick my heels, brood, percolate, hibernate and wait for something to happen. (72)

Mining the contradictions and tensions of the US/Mexico border, "where the Third World grates against the first and bleeds," Anzaldúa (1987) theorizes psychological, sexual, and spiritual borderlands that operate in many geographies (3). As a Chicana, feminist lesbian, Anzaldúa uses the metaphor of the border to theorize multiple axes of difference. The Borderlands are "physically present wherever two or more cultures edge each other, where people of different races occupy the same territory, where under, lower, middle and upper classes touch, where the space between two individuals shrinks with intimacy" (ix). A stunning example of intersectional feminism, Anzaldúa's *Borderlands/La Frontera: The New Mestiza* charts a consciousness defined by its ability to cross and straddle borders, to hold contradiction, and embrace ambiguity. Anzaldúa describes this consciousness as "alien" and "mutable, more malleable" (77). The bearer of such a consciousness moves beyond "a counterstance" reacting to dominant ideologies, finds healing, and arrives in "a wholly new and separate territory" (79).

The articulation of consciousness has been a rich ground on which to explore difference, power, and the self. Chela Sandoval (1991) theorizes differential consciousness in "US Third World Feminism:

The Theory and Method of Oppositional Consciousness in the Postmodern World." Heralding a new subject position, the enactment of this consciousness is

> mobile—not nomadic but rather cinematographic: a kinetic motion that maneuvers, poetically transfigures, and orchestrates while demanding alienation, perversion, and reformation in both spectators and practitioners. (x)

Literary critic Vèvè A. Clark (2009) argues for the development of marasa consciousness as a way of reading contemporary African diasporic literature. This rich terrain of thinking about consciousness provides creative writers with tools for character analysis, critical reflection on our identities as writers, and a complex vocabulary for encountering one another in the workshop space.

Counternarrative

Stories shape our understanding of the world. We think in stories. "To narrate," Judith Summerfield notes, "is, according to the word's Greek etymology, to know" (180).

We tell ourselves a story every time we interpret an event or occurrence, every time we explain actions or results. Some of the stories we tell ourselves come from larger, "grand" narratives, including narratives that define what "progress" looks like, or narratives about what is "good" or "right" or "natural." Some grand narratives are identified by name: the "American Dream," for example, is a narrative that says freedom and success are available to all through hard work within a capitalist system; "terra nullius" is another narrative that considers another's land to be a vast space of "nothingness" that is there for the taking. "Terra nullius" was part of a grand narrative of Manifest Destiny that told the European-descended colonist in North America that this "nothingness" was his entitlement, inevitably and rightfully.

Grand narratives have shaped, motivated, and justified innumerable decisions and actions; they are powerful forces in society—hence the term "grand," which Jean-François Lyotard made common parlance for theorists seeking to understand the relationships of power in culture. Lyotard argued in *The Postmodern Condition* (1979) that all knowledge is contingent because all knowledge is story.

We could tell our stories differently, and telling the story differently would create different effects. Consider narratives in Eurocentric Western history that have held that accumulation of wealth, control, and power are the highest and most necessary values for human flourishing. Such cultural narratives have supported colonialism. These are narratives about supremacy and inferiority, rather than reciprocity and reverence for difference. We find narratives that cast Western knowledge as absolute and "objective," as "the way things are."

For those who "live the privilege of believing the official story," as M. Jacqui Alexander puts it in *Pedagogies of Crossing* (2), the cultural messages that we receive may become invisible. They may seem to be a "matter of fact," "commonsense," or "truth." Donald Morton and Mas'ud Zavarzadeh, in "The Cultural Politics of the Fiction Workshop," explain the naturalization of dominant stories in these terms: "The socially dominant class has the final say in the designation of what is 'real' (what 'makes sense') and what is 'non-real' (what is 'nonsense') in a society" (157). In turn, the lived realities of those who do not fit within the socially dominant class are marginalized as "nonsense" and inconsequential.

When a narrative presents itself as transparent "reality" and insists upon its objectivity, the contingency of that narrative (i.e., the fact that the narrative serves a particular group and is of a particular place and time) becomes hidden. This is how narratives of Western knowledge come to seem as natural as the earth's rotation or revolution around the sun, a "given" that we don't attempt to change.

These narratives are not "givens." They are human inventions. But the dominant narratives take hold in a society, and these narratives have power behind them. They are narratives that win the assent of people through indirect and implicit means, pervading how people think of themselves and each other in the world.

In an interview with Bill Moyers from 1990, Toni Morrison defined the term "master narrative," (which is akin to the terms "dominant narrative" and "grand narrative") in this way: "The Master Narrative is whatever ideological script that is being imposed by the people in authority on everybody else." She continues, explaining how the master narrative "has a certain point of view," and she provides an illustrative example: Speaking of girls of color, Morrison observes, "when those little girls see that the most prized gift they can receive at Christmas time is this little white doll, that's the Master Narrative speaking: *this is beautiful, this is lovely, and you're not it.*" As Morrison notes, the dominant narratives that circulate in our world reinforce hierarchies by assigning value to only certain people, creating and sustaining hierarchies and forms of supremacy. These hierarchies are contingent; they are not givens, but rather they are inventions that serve some at the great expense and harm of many.

Every assumption we make about what reality is, or what reality should be, is born out of the narratives we have learned. Every stereotype that we have about another person is a narrative that we've learned. Every time we expect a certain set of things from a person (say, expecting that a man will be a better leader than a woman), we are drawing upon dominant narratives to tell us what to expect from the story of our own and another's existence.

In her TED Talk "The Danger of a Single Story," Chimamanda Ngozi Adichie speaks about the "single stories" that she has encountered and has herself held. These "single stories," or dominant narratives, limit and reduce what people can know about themselves and each other. Adichie illustrates how these "single stories" are fundamentally alienating and harmful. She shows us this by telling a series of stories that don't fit into dominant narratives. Her talk ends with the hopeful possibility: "When we reject the single story, when we realize that there is never a single story about any place, we regain a kind of paradise."

Adichie's words are important for writers to remember, as every time we sit down to write we are in danger of repeating the "dangers of a single story." If we don't take the time to be reflective about the dominant narratives that may be operating in the stories we tell on the page, we may inadvertently find ourselves reinforcing harmful narratives. These narratives are "in the air" (4), as Joanna Russ says in her essay "What Can a Heroine Do?" (1972). We breathe these narratives in and out every day. It takes deliberate, mindful attention to be able to breathe differently, as it were—to slow down enough to realize that our otherwise automatic "uptake" of these narratives doesn't need to be automatic, as Anis Bawarshi notes in "Between Genres: Uptake, Memory, and U.S. Public Discourse on Israel-Palestine."

We can choose a different story. We don't have to take up the one that is most available in our cultural milieu. This kind of deliberateness requires that writers participate in "effortful processing" (Johnson 2018) and do the work of asking: what characters occupy what roles in my story? Am I falling into common patterns of representation that reinforce dominant narratives and stereotypes? Am I representing the world in such a way that says "this is the right way," or am I opening up new possibilities with close attention to the complexities of human experience?

Counternarratives are not necessarily narratives that refute, point-for-point, dominant ideas by constructing antithetical stories. Instead, counternarratives break open dominant narratives, exposing them for what they are: contingent stories that serve some at the expense of more. Some counternarratives are forms of counter-memory, or stories that transform history through suppressed or subjugated knowledge. Counternarratives are a form of counter-discourse—a term often attributed to Richard Terdiman that is used to describe "symbolic resistance," or ways of countering hegemony through language. By "hegemony," we mean the perceptions, ideas, beliefs that have become naturalized or "common sense" as they serve dominant members of society. Counter-discourse, counternarrative, and counter-memory pose a challenge to common assumptions. The work of the counternarrative is not to construct a new version of a master narrative to replace an old; the counternarrative instead works to question "official stories," and to expose them for who and what they serve. The counternarrative may do this by speaking to experiences that are left outside of the master narrative, offering epistemologies that are occluded or castigated by what is dominant. Counternarratives are a way of countering epistemic injustice, therefore.

The counternarrative insists upon the question "who does it serve?" when thinking about the stories that circulate in our world. We can bring this question to our work as writers. W. Kamau Bell provides an example of what it means to ask this question in more specific terms, noting that "when art sets racism in the past, no matter how good it is, it allows white people in the audience (and others) to say to themselves 'Wow! That racism sure was bad way back then!' It's what happens when people go see *12 Years a Slave*. My response is always," Bell continues, "Yeah, you wanna know another time when racism was bad? Earlier today."

What stories are you reinforcing when you write? Are you reinforcing stories that present racism, sexism, ableism, xenophobia, homophobia, and other forms of oppression as something that happened in the past? Are you reinforcing stories that cast white people or people who occupy a dominant subject-position as the saviors of the hapless "other"? Are you reinforcing stereotypes, or harmful ideas? Are you recirculating the stories that are "in the air," or are you doing the difficult work of excavating your own assumptions, your own adopted master narratives? Are you doing the internal work of coming to terms with your identity and what it means for you to write from the positionality you have, and the histories to which you are inevitably tied?

Asking these questions can help us to think differently about the common mantras that circulate in workshop conversations. The idea, for example, that you should "write what you know" becomes challenging when we consider the role master narratives may have in shaping what we know. This is what Claudia Rankine and Beth Loffreda point to when, in their introduction to *The Racial Imaginary*, they warn, "It should be difficult to write what one knows—and if it is too easy, it is worth asking if that is because one is reproducing conventions and assumptions rewarded by the marketplaces of literatures."

AnaLouise Keating calls upon writers to question "status-quo stories," which she defines as the "worldviews that normalize and naturalize the existing social system, values, and standards so entirely that they prevent us from imagining the possibility of change" (35). Keating sees value in "revisionist mythmaking," or the rewriting of status-quo stories, as "an important tool to effect transformation on multiple levels—ranging from our psychic lives to our social structures—and beyond. Revisionist mythmaking can take a variety of forms: we can entirely reject the existing stories, rewrite portions of them, retell them from different perspectives, recover alternative versions that have been lost *(or that never before existed),* and create new myths" (112). She continues, "When we change our focus by defining these status-quo stories *as* status-quo stories—rather than as factual information about reality—we can reread them from additional perspectives. We can recognize their limitations and explore new options—which might range from revising the status-quo stories to entirely retelling them to moving beyond them and writing new stories" (170). This is the work of the counternarrative.

Diaspora

The word "diaspora," a Greek term meaning "to disperse," was originally taken up to describe the experience of Jewish people after the Babylonian captivity of 586 BC (*OED*). A diaspora is a dispersal of people, sometimes violent and forced, but possibly voluntary, from their homeland into new regions. The field of diaspora theory and explorations of diaspora in creative writing have now expanded to encompass many different groups, including the Irish diaspora, Palestinian diaspora, African diaspora, and more. Diaspora theory engages themes of memory, home, trauma, identity, violence, and the "forced scattering" of populations (Sudbury 2004). Theorizing diaspora is central to understanding colonialism.

Robin Cohen (2008) argues that diaspora studies has gone through four phases: (1) the classic use of the term to explain the Jewish experience, (2) beginning in the 1980s, the expansion of the use of the concept to describe the experiences of a variety of groups, (3) a wave of social constructionist and postmodernist critique of the concept of diaspora, as articulated previously. These theorists destabilized the notions of homeland and ethnic/religious community, focusing on the complexity of identity, and finally (4) a reconsolidation of the concept of diaspora, incorporating phrase three critiques, characterized by "a requestioning and more sophisticated understanding of shifts in the homeland—diaspora relationship, the ways in which a diaspora is mobilized and how diaspora studies connect to post-colonial studies" (12).

As Ashcroft, Griffiths, and Tiffin (2013) write, "Colonialism itself was a radically diasporic movement, involving the temporary or permanent dispersion and settlement of millions of Europeans over the entire world" (61). As these settlers established plantations and agricultural colonies, labor was needed to grow food for the metropole. The result of this was systems of enslavement across the Americas. The primarily West African peoples forcibly removed from their homelands and made to work for the profit of Europeans became diasporic peoples, crafting hybridized identities which incorporated and syncretized aspects of their traditional cultures and newfound elements. The descendants of colonial diasporic formations

have developed their own distinctive cultures which both preserve and often extend and develop their originary cultures. Creolized versions of their own practices evolved, modifying (and being modified by) indigenous cultures with which they thus came into contact. The development of diasporic cultures necessarily questions essentialist models, interrogating the ideology of a unified, 'natural' cultural norm, one that underpins the centre/margin model of colonialist discourse. It also questions the simpler kinds of theories of nativism which suggest that decolonization can be affected by a recovery or reconstruction of pre-colonial societies. (Ashcroft et al., 62)

Diaspora studies have been an incredibly generative site for inquiry and literary production, generating notions of creolization, syncretization, and hybridity.

Diaspora became an increasingly layered nexus of scholarly work as a result of the popularity of intellectuals associated with the Centre for Contemporary Cultural Studies at the University of Birmingham (Edwards 2001). Avtar Brah is an important innovator of thinking on diaspora. Brah (1996) develops the concept of diaspora space "as a conceptual category [which] is 'inhabited' not only by those who have migrated and their descendants but equally by those who are constructed and represented as Indigenous. In other words, the concept of diaspora space (as opposed to that of diaspora) includes the entanglement of genealogies of dispersion with those of 'staying put'" (Brah 181). Brah shows how the cultural hybridity characteristic of diasporic populations is a key feature of all cultural practice.

Studying the literature of diaspora requires attention to the complexities of identity, how dispersal from one's homeland or original location continues to structure the present and how the process of dispersal—whether the result of enslavement, colonialism, migration for work, or political exclusion—is violent and chaotic, but also productive of liberatory potentialities. Dispersal often requires redefinition of the Self and the formulation of hybrid identities. Creative writing has been a central site for exploration of identity and diaspora. Salman Rushdie writes in *Imaginary Homelands* (2012) of a haunting "sense of loss" and "urge to reclaim" that exiles, emigrants, and expatriates might experience. The need to "look back," he writes, is complex and multivalenced. To look back "gives rise to profound uncertainties," Rushdie observes, about the possibility of "reclaiming precisely the thing that was lost." There is the haunting sense that all one can do is "create fictions, not actual cities or villages, but invisible ones, imaginary homelands" (10). Rushdie's writing gives one example of the struggle over homeland, identity, and hybridity.

Hybridity is a well-worn term in postcolonial theory, referring to the creation of new cultural practices within zones of colonial contact. Homi Bhabha's work is often cited in reference to the concept of hybridity. In *The Location of Culture*, Bhabha defines hybridity as "a problematic of colonial representations ... that reverses the effects of the colonist disavowal, so that other 'denied' knowledges enter upon the dominant discourse and estrange the basis of its authority" (156). Bhabha uses the conceptual vocabulary of a "third space of enunciation" to argue that notions of a pure or essentialized original culture is always a fiction. In Jonathan Rutherford's words, "all forms of culture are continually in a process of hybridity" (211). Perhaps all identity and cultural practice is, as Rushdie puts it, "haunted by some sense of loss" and characterized by the creation of fictions.

Narrating relations of time, space, and violent dispersal has been a central project of diaspora studies focused on people of African descent. As Sudbury (2004) writes, "Constant retellings of forced relocation via the Middle Passage, and subsequent migrations in response to war, impoverishment and racial terrorism, place a shared memory of time gone by at the center of black collective identity" (154).

Paul Gilroy theorizes the concept of the "Black Atlantic" to name the transnational linkages unifying Black cultures. He uses the image of the ship to interrogate the potentialities of identities spanning two or more points of connection, showing that "the economic and political framework of the Atlantic region as a whole, ha[s] been determined in large part by the linkages formed in that first era of mercantilism and expansion when the principal cargo was the bodies of black Africans" (qtd. in Ashcroft et al., 22). Gilroy moves the Black radical tradition out from under the boundaries of the nation-state, showing how notions of Britishness are constituted by the exclusion of blackness and that Black cultural production relies on sophisticated experiences of transnational cultural exchange.

Rabab Abdulhadi (2003) explores the complexities of "going home" for people in the political exile of the Palestinian diaspora. The Israeli Law of Return grants citizenship automatically to any Jewish people upon arriving in Israel, while the indigenous Palestinian population continues to be exiled from their homeland following the 1948 expulsion, known as the *nakba* or catastrophe. She writes, "Going home is transformed into a politically charged project in which the struggle for self-identification, self-determination, freedom, and dignity becomes as salient as the physical and mental safety of one's 'informants,' and the power differential in the production and reproduction of knowledge. 'Where is home?' is a question that lies at the center of Palestinian precarious experience" (89).

Azar Nafisi narrates the complexities of home in her memoir *Reading Lolita in Tehran*, writing:

I wrote, rather dramatically, to an American friend: "You ask me what it means to be irrelevant? The feeling is akin to visiting your old house as a wandering ghost with unfinished business. Imagine going back: the structure is familiar, but the door is now metal instead of wood, the walls have been painted a garish pink, the easy chair you loved so much is gone. … This is your house, and it is not. And you are no longer relevant to this house, to its walls and doors and floors; you are not seen." (169)

Increasingly the concept of "diaspora" is being taken up in broader terms. Scholars working at the intersection of diaspora studies and queer theory have increasingly shown how new experiences and ideas of gender and sexuality are produced through the conditions of geographical mobility. There is a queerness to diaspora which is increasingly reflected in the writings of transnational queer subjects. As Meg Wesling (2008) writes, "It is the diasporic queer subject in particular who is called upon to bear witness to the political, material, familial, and intellectual transformations of globalization …. [framed as] the exemplary subject of globalization, in order to posit an analogy between queerness as that which subverts gender normativity, and diaspora as that which troubles geographic and national stability" (31). Diaspora theory has provided a route for scholars of ethnic literature and others to interrogate the "transnational identities" of those living between, alongside, or in several cultural spaces or communities.

Disability

Think about the ways you write the human body. How are the bodies of your characters described in your work? What do those bodies do? What is assumed about those bodies?

Maybe your initial response to the above questions is to say that your work doesn't much concern itself with the human body, yet Eli Clare, author of *Exile and Pride*, makes it clear that ultimately, "We cannot ignore the body itself: the sensory, mostly non-verbal experience of our hearts and lungs, muscles and tendons, telling us and the world who we are" (150). Writers need to be cognizant of the messages they may, at times unconsciously, be reinforcing by how they represent, or fail to represent, disability in their writing. Creative writers produce literary images that shape perception and understanding.

Think about the common patterns or tropes you find in literature that represents disability. Perhaps you think of narratives where a secondary character becomes "enfreaked," a word David Hevey uses to describe the representation of individuals as "freaks"—a type of "othering" that produces spectacle. Perhaps you think of secondary characters who are rendered as mere symbols for something else—their lived experience becoming less important than what they stand for, their complex existence summed up in a simple message. This phenomenon of rendering the human as a symbol is common in literature. As Kristen Harmon and Jennifer Nelson note in their introduction to *Deaf American Prose*,

> The few deaf characters in literary English—written by mostly hearing writers—are more often presented as woebegone or existential metaphors for the human (i.e., hearing) condition. In general, deaf characters as written by non-signers are used to metaphorize the status of the outsider, the alienated person in a modern world, the naive innocent, the ignorant person incapable of receiving instruction or salvation, and other concepts. (xii)

When you recall common presentations of disability you might notice certain trends: narratives that describe a protagonist who overcomes an impairment, often through extraordinary means, might be commonplace in your mental list of representations of disability. This narrative Eli Clare calls the "supercrip" story, and it is one of the dominant images of disabled people. Clare identifies a number of problems with supercrip stories, as they "rely upon the perception that disability and achievement contradict each other and that any disabled person who overcomes this contradiction is heroic" (9). To reinforce a notion that disability and achievement contradict each other is to reinforce a kind of prejudice. This prejudice may manifest in different ways in different genres and narrative forms. Focusing on speculative fictions that imagine a future world, Alison Kafer observes an implication in future-oriented literatures that "disability is seen as the sign of no future or at least of no good future" (3). This is a focus of Kafer's book

Feminist, Queer, Crip, which interrogates the role of disability in our imagined futures. In the article "Debating Feminist Futures," which is included in the book *Feminist Disability Studies* (2011), Kafer notes how the depiction of fictional worlds where disability is removed through technological advancements "treats disability as temporary and assumes that disability destroys the quality of life, that a better life precludes disability, and that disability can and should be 'fixed' through technological invention" (234).

These common narratives risk what Tobin Siebers in *Disability Aesthetics* calls "disqualification," an oppressive symbolic process in which individuals are removed from the ranks of quality human beings. Siebers notes that an "aesthetics of disqualification presents in almost every sphere of human influence" (28).

Working against this tendency, disability studies has sought to, in Kafer's words, "pluralize the ways we understand bodily instability" (7), in order to undo such forms of disqualification. Troubling the distinction between "disabled" and "nondisabled," disability studies interrogates "the political nature of the framing of disability" (Kafer 6). Sami Schalk further defines the field of disability studies in *Bodyminds Reimagined*: "Disability studies is the interdisciplinary investigation of (dis)ability as a socially constructed phenomenon and systemic social discourse which determines how bodyminds and behaviors are labeled, valued, represented, and treated" (3). In other words, "disability" is an interpretive fame and a construct that should be continually interrogated.

Disability is a construct. To say this, however, is not to ignore the lived, material effects of bodily impairment. Allan G. Johnson clarifies this point in "The Social Construction of Difference": When we say that "disability and nondisability are socially constructed," we don't "mean that the difference between having or not having full use of your legs is somehow 'made up' without any objective reality. It does mean, however, that how people notice and label and think about such differences and how they treat other people as a result depends entirely on ideas contained in a system's culture" (16). Johnson is calling us to think about the language we use to describe and define disability. This involves taking a critical eye to the common narratives about disability outlined above; it also entails thinking about the vocabulary we use to label and categorize.

In a chapter devoted to the question of the language we use, Eli Clare in *Exile and Pride* writes: "I think about language. I often call nondisabled people able-bodied, or when I'm feeling confrontational, *temporarily* able-bodied. But if I call myself disabled in order to describe how the ableist world treats me as a person with cerebral palsy, then shouldn't I call nondisabled people *enabled?*" (82). This change in the language—using the term "enabled," rather than "able-bodied"—destabilizes common notions about disability, emphasizing the ways that certain embodiments are privileged and "enabled" by the structures of society. The word "enabled," in Clare's terms, "locates the condition of being nondisabled, not in the non-disabled body, but in the world's reaction to that body. This is not a semantic game" (82).

The language we use can reveal the world we've built, where the assumptions of this world might otherwise be hidden. We make assumptions in how we build buildings, in how we render reading material, in how we draft medical policies, in how we represent the world in media. Some people are "enabled" by societal choices in architecture, document design, medical policy, cultural representation, and so on. Tobin Siebers provides an example in *Disability Aesthetics*, noting how "aesthetic judgments about the built environment remain unquestioned when architects make the case against accessible designs on the grounds that access produces ugly buildings, despite the fact that those buildings called beautiful are fashioned to suppress the disabled body" (80–81). If we can count an inaccessible architectural design aesthetically valuable, Siebers argues, then our aesthetic theory exhibits prejudice. To what extent does Siebers's observation about architecture also apply to literature? To what extent do we operate with aesthetic theories that value what marginalizes, excludes, and disadvantages? Siebers is interested in the ways that disability may be an aesthetic value in itself, one that can counter the prejudicial nature of previously held theories of architecture, art, and literature.

Clare and Siebers show us how some are actively *disabled* by societal choices. This term is a verb, not a noun. The lack of a wheelchair ramp for that theater stage, the lack of universally designed materials in this classroom, the lack of storylines for diverse protagonists of different abilities in our films, novels, and stories—all of these operated *to disable*, and this is what is meant by the term "ableism." Ableism is the "material, social, legal conditions" that people with disabilities experience (Clare 3). As a form of oppression, ableism includes "lack of access, lack of employment, lack of education, lack of personal attendant services … stereotypes and attitudes" (3). Clare states in clear terms: "It is ableism that needs the cure, not our bodies" (122).

Some authors have made a deliberate effort to counter the ableism of literary studies. Crip aesthetics has emerged in recent decades, with J.L. Baird's 1983 article in *Kaleidoscope*, which critiqued elements of poetry written about disability that he surveyed. This is only one of many formative moments in the conversation, and there is no one point of origin. We should be skeptical of origin stories, especially as they may privilege one person's or group's contributions over another's. Chris Bell's "Introducing White Disability Studies: A Modest Proposal," published in 2006, is another important point in the timeline of disability studies, as this piece of scholarship called the field to account for the white-centrism of its conversations. An intersectional approach to disability studies considers how multiple forms of oppression work together to create structures of inequality. Sami Schalk explains how

> the social system of (dis)ability has a different impact on and meaning for ... populations due to race. A crip theory approach to race and disability studies requires an expansion of the category of disability to include illness, disease, and secondary health effects. This is because people of color and the poor are more likely to have experiences on the borders of or outside of able-bodiedness due to violence and failures of society to provide access to affordable, quality insurance, housing, and medical care. (10)

Three years after the publication of the Baird article, the book *Toward Solomon's Mountain* was released, a collection that is sometimes cited as the "birth of disability poetry as a genre" (Northen 18). These anthologies that are expressly conscious of questions of ability are significant contributions that writers should know well, but we should also remember, as Jennifer Bartlett does in the introduction to *Beauty Is a Verb: The New Poetry of Disability*, that "most poets could be looked at through a disability lens" (16).

Bartlett is here citing Michael Davidson in troubling the divide between disabled and non-disabled poets and writers, but the point has been made by many theorists. As Kafer notes, illness and disability are part of what make us human.

Thinking about disability in creative writing means becoming more conscious of the assumptions we make about literary production, becoming more attentive to the language that we use to describe our writing. (Consider, for example, the emphasis placed on "voice" in creative writing.) Thinking about disability in creative writing means destabilizing the cultural fantasy of the normative body. It means considering the embodied nature of writing and reading processes; it means seeking to create accessibility in the texts we circulate and produce.

Accessibility is something different from accommodation; accessibility is about presenting something that all can engage, across difference—in contrast to merely retooling an otherwise inaccessible norm on a case-by-case basis to "accommodate" someone's needs. Accessibility means learning about universal design, and encouraging writers, publishers, and teachers alike to utilize these principles.

These are just some of the ways that creative writers can come to account for our own perpetuation of *enabling* systems that don't enable all.

Emotion

As creative writers, we work with and in emotive language. But exactly what is "emotive language"? What is emotion? "Emotion" encapsulates a vast range of meanings—so much so that Paul Griffiths has argued we should do away with the term "emotion" altogether and replace it with a more precise set of terms.

Think about the metaphors that you use to describe emotion. Perhaps you've thought of how emotions can be "bottled up inside" or how someone may seem "ready to burst" into tears. These metaphors tell us something about popular conceptions of emotional experience. They rest upon an understanding of emotion as an internal, fixed state of feeling; they emphasize an internal/external dichotomy.

When we think of the writing process, we may similarly rely on an internal/external dichotomy—speaking of how writing enables us to get our emotions "out." This idea of emotional expression through writing assumes an individual internal emotional state that gets projected outward in language.

Theorists like Sara Ahmed question this idea about emotion, complicating cultural tropes of the isolated, reflective artist who finds an external form for private experience. Ahmed proposes that the artist composes within what she calls an "affective economy." The artist makes certain emotions "stick," but this "affective language" exists only in circulation. Emotion is not something one *has*. It is not something one can possess. Rather, we experience emotion within shifting affective economies.

What Ahmed posits is something similar to Denise Riley's theory of emotion and language in *Impersonal Passion*. For Riley, all language is soaked in affect. Affect "seeps from the very form of the words" (Riley 2). This seeping can't be fully staunched by intention: "There is a tangible affect in language which stands somewhat apart from the expressive intentions of an individual speaker," Riley writes (5)—a point echoed by Ahmed as she insists that emotions cannot be fully pre-determined.

While some theorists (Sara Ahmed and Teresa Brennan, for example) use the terms "affect" and "emotion" interchangeably, others (such as Brian Massumi) make a distinction. For some—especially those who are influenced by the theories of Gilles Deleuze or Silvan Tomkins, two very different theorists who come together in the work of contemporary emotion studies—the term "affect" denotes a pre-linguistic charge, intensity, or energy while "emotion" is located in the realm of the symbolic order, the realm of meaning, the realm of belief and subjective evaluation. Affect is considered to be impersonal, non-intentional, and not "ownable or recognizable" (Massumi 28), whereas emotion is what John Protevi calls "the subjective capture of affect" (54).

The subject of emotion is much debated and theorized across the disciplines—in neurobiology, anthropology, sociology, psychology, history, the humanities, etc. Some of the key topics of debate in emotion studies include the relationship between emotion and belief, between emotion and cognition, between emotion and language, between emotion and the body, between emotion and ethics, between emotion and culture.

Theorists approach these questions by thinking of emotion in cognitive, neurobiological, cultural-constructivist, and ecological terms. *Cognitive* theories of emotion focus on the relationship between emotion and judgment or belief. *Neurobiological* approaches to emotion seek to track universal "basic" emotions that are common to members of our species, and possibly other species as well. *Cultural-constructionist* theories examine how aspects of culture, including language, shape emotion, holding that all we experience and understand is filtered through language and culture. Emotion, in this view, is tied to social practices and interpreted within a cultural framework; therefore, emotions are not universal, fixed, or solely internal. *Ecological* theories, in turn, hold that "emotions are what link us, as individuals, to our surroundings" (25), as Kay Milton notes in a chapter of the book *Mixed Emotions*. The ecological model critiques the anthropocentrism of other schools of thought, and notes how our understandings are built from the "raw material" of the more-than-human environment (31). For Milton, perception is an ecological as well as social process, and emotion is part of perception—in forming memories of the environment and attaching to aspects of the environment that help us to adapt and learn (32).

Some writers are influenced by more than one of these schools of thought on emotion. David Konstan, for example, asserts that "complex emotions, at least, are constituted as much by culture as by biology" (17). John Protevi also joins the social and the somatic in his account of emotion; he writes that "emotions, while not genetically determined, do reliably develop provided that the basic elements of human contexts (such as nutrition and care) are present" (24). At the same time, "socialization practices instill 'emotion scripts' that indicate culturally specific forms of acceptable performance of emotions" (Protevi 24–25).

Each of the four schools of thought described above has influenced literary studies. Patrick Colm Hogan brings the neurobiological approach to his theory of "affective narratology." Martha Nussbaum employs a cognitivist approach, arguing in *The Therapy of Desire* that "emotions are forms of intentional awareness" (80). In her book *Upheavals of Thought*, Nussbaum analyzes pity in ancient tragedy, in order to argue that emotion has an important place in ethical thought. Nussbaum says that "narrative emotions"—those emotions that literary texts prompt in their audiences—can instruct us toward an attention to suffering. She turns to tragedy and other tragic narratives because "such works of art promote compassion in their audience by inviting both empathy and judgment ... They also work more directly to construct the constituent judgments of compassion" (*Upheavals* 351).

The cultural constructionist approach has also generated useful concepts for literary practitioners; one such concept is Moldoveneau and Nohria's term "master passion," which takes the concept of the "master narrative" (see the chapter on counternarrative in the present text) and applies it to emotion. Examples of master passions are envy and anger, which are culturally constructed experiences that are played out in narratives of the self's relationship to the world. Since we are always narrating our experience, these socially generated master passions "create what reality 'feels like' for us" (Moldoveneau and Nohria 3, 32). The master passions "create their own 'realities' by lighting up our experiences in different ways" (56). The concept of the master passion allows us to theorize how one's felt sense of reality is conditioned by hegemonic, normative cultural understandings. The concept of "master passion" provides us a way of thinking about the relationship between emotion and normativity.

All of the schools of thought have limitations, and our understanding of the relationship between literature and emotion should be cognizant of the risks and possibilities of each paradigm. In thinking about trauma specifically, but in a way that applies to the relationship between emotion and literature more broadly, Maruška Svašek warns that emotions—including those involved with trauma—"must neither be reduced to individual psychobiological malfunctioning, nor be simplified as purely sociocultural phenomenon" ("Chosen Trauma" 208).

The relationship between literature and emotion has long been theorized in the aesthetic tradition. Victor Hugo famously answered the question, "What indeed is a poet?" with the description of "A man [*sic*] who feels strongly and expresses his feelings in a more expressive language" (qtd. in Beardsley). Tolstoy similarly emphasized emotion as definitive of the artist and art: he writes, "Art begins when a man, with the purpose of communicating to other people a feeling he once experienced, calls it up again within himself and expresses it by external signs" (107). For Tolstoy, art should promote communion and unity among people, and this communion should be brought about through fellow-feeling. That is, through art, one can receive "through hearing or sight the expressions of another man's feelings" and become "capable of experiencing the same feelings as the man who expresses them" (107).

In the Western aesthetic tradition, the artist has been variously conceived of as a creator of forms that "instruct and delight" and shape readers' hearts (Horace); as one who possesses a delicacy of imagination necessary for finer emotions (Hume); as a "Man of Achievement" imbued with negative capability or "being in uncertainties" (Keats); as one who vacates an expressive personality to place emotion in correlative things (T.S. Eliot). These conceptions—which represent just a sampling of ideas we find in one Eurocentric, male-dominated aesthetic tradition—ask artists to shape themselves in certain ways, to cultivate certain emotional dispositions or stances toward the world. These aesthetic theories advocate ways of being; they extend to the artist's whole life—in both ethical and emotional orientations.

There is a politics at work in these propositions about the relationship between emotion and ethics. Several thinkers from within and outside of the aesthetic tradition focus on the relationship between emotion and power. Allison Jaggar proposes the term "emotional hegemony" (130) to describe what Lisa Langstraat identifies as "the processes through which dominant groups struggle to regulate the epistemic potential of emotions, thereby determining which emotional states are valued and which are mistrusted in specific contexts. Emotional hegemony is effective only insofar as it wins our consent by naturalizing that which is saturated with power relations" (300).

An artist may work upon emotional hegemony in producing art that calls us into a new relationship with the emotional conditions of our world. As Elba Rosario Sánchez writes in the essay "Cartohistografía: Continente de una voz,"

> Words and writing have been a way to deal with the powerful emotions that come with injustice. [...] The anger I have felt has, in fact, collaborated many a time with my writing and propelled me to search for the strongest, most powerful words I can fuse together to name or question a harsh reality. In my experience, anger has the potential to generate good; it has moved me enough to try to change some wrong, to speak about that wrong out loud; it has pushed me to do something. (50)

There is political potential in speaking and writing anger at injustice. However, simply having an emotion is not equivalent to enacting political change—a warning that is reinforced by both Sara Ahmed and Lauren Berlant. As Sara Ahmed notes in *The Cultural Politics of Emotion*, the question of "having" or "not having" emotion cannot in any way be the ground of ethics or justice (195). Or, in Lauren Berlant's terms, "the repetition of empathic events does not in itself create change" (166). Berlant worries that an ethics grounded in compassion, sympathy, or another privileged or "true feeling" can replace "the ethical imperative toward social transformation" and the material righting of inequities with "a passive world of private thoughts, leanings, and gestures" (41). Both Berlant and Ahmed are concerned with the social hierarchies that may be implicit in understandings of ethical emotions like empathy, compassion, pity, etc. (i.e., the view, expressed by thinkers such as Rousseau and Adam Smith, that cultivating sympathy will cultivate ethics). Ahmed shows how maintaining a "distinction between the subject and object of feeling" (193)—as in a distinction between the one who pities and the one who is pitiable—can reinforce a patronizing and hierarchical social relation that maintains an inequitable status quo.

Nonetheless, there may be, Ahmed suggests, certain emotional configurations coincident with activism and material change. Ahmed notes how happiness may signal an acceptance of the status quo, whereas unhappiness stirs things up. Unhappy emotions are, in this sense, active. They are "creative responses" to conditions (*Promise of Happiness* 217), and they are ripe with potential to instigate change.

An understanding of the politics of emotion is important for creative writers. An understanding of theories of emotion allows us to contextualize literature that attempts to be sympathetic or compassionate toward its subject matter. Thinking through the politics of emotion at work in each piece of literature becomes an important aspect of considering identity in literature.

Emotion is one of the lenses through which we evaluate literature. Perhaps the words "sentimental" and "melodramatic" come to mind—two terms that are often used in workshop that belie a value system related to emotion. These terms have long been part of creative writing discourse. Even creative writing craft textbooks from the early twentieth century had something to say about these terms. Joseph Berg Esenwein's short-story handbook, published in 1918, which draws upon Winchester's *Principles of Literary Criticism*, has the following to say about sentimentality:

The hackneyed, vulgar, prurient and bestial treatment of love and the passions in the short-story cannot be too strongly condemned, particularly when found in a periodical for home circulation. Surely the sincere story-writer must feel a sense of his responsibly and avoid the cheap sentimentalism which, in spite of its undeserved popularity, is as ephemeral as it is inartistic. 'All forms of sentimentalism in literature,' says Winchester, 'result from the endeavor to excite the emotions of pathos or affection without adequate cause. Emotions thus easily aroused or consciously indulged for their own sake, have something hollow about them. The emotion excited by the true artist is grounded upon the deep truths of human life.' (184)

When an evaluative system employs emotion to tell us what is "good" or worthy in literature, we should be mindful of the ways that power relations may be at work. Whose literatures are most likely to be called sentimental? If it's the case that literature written by women or the literatures associated with "mass culture" are most likely to be called sentimental, then what does this indicate? Are conceptions of the "sentimental" a way of maintaining hierarchies within the regime of literary value?

The sentimental is often associated with "imprecision" in literature, or a lack of objectivity. Borrowing from Rilke, Dobyns defines sentimentality as the mode in which artists present something as if they were saying "'I love this' instead of 'here it is'" (354). The fantasy of neutrality and objectivity in the presentation of "here it is" is a fantasy that belongs to those who have the privilege of seeing their worldview as normative and neutral. There is no objective and neutral way of presenting something "as it is." We are always rendering our subjects with investments, desires, orientations saying "I love this" or "I don't love this". It is only when one's investments match the dominant ideology that one can appear to be saying only "here it is."

This phenomenon is related to the issue of "emotional decorum." As Sara Ahmed observes in *The Cultural Politics of Emotion*, "Some emotions are 'elevated' as signs of cultivation, whilst others remain 'lower' as signs of weakness" in different cultures and at different times (3). For instance, melancholy was, Marjorie Garber notes, "a highly desired emotion in the early modern period" of Anglophone European thought and literature. Melancholy was "associated with art, learning, and privilege" (141). In your investigation of literary history, you may have encountered the heroic, masculinist, unhappy revolutionary "whose suffering is a gift to the world" (Ahmed, *Promise of Happiness* 169). Such formulations, in elevating the emotional orientations of some, may in turn disparage the sensibilities of others. Consider, for example, the silencing experienced by those rendered "angry" and therefore irrational, not to be listened to. Construing emotion as indecorous becomes a warrant for hostility to the one who speaks of the anger produced by injustice. The angry, sentimental, or melodramatic writer may be dismissed as being in violation of a system of emotional decorum that serves the status quo. How we regard and value emotion in literature has much to do with questions of identity therefore.

Essentialism

Essentialism holds that any being, object, or concept possesses certain fixed, or "essential," properties by which it is defined and without which it would not be what it is. This concept is a central preoccupation of Western thought. In *The Metaphysics*, Aristotle articulates an epistemological position which in many ways inaugurates this doctrine in Western thought. He argues that it is the fundamental objective of scientific inquiry to uncover the essences of things in order to detail why they exist and how they contribute to an overarching taxonomy of the universe. Essentialism has been challenged by scholars across the disciplines. As Max Weber famously said, "For scientific truth is but that which aspires to be true for all those who *want* scientific truth" (qtd. in Fuchs 2009).

Postmodern criticism, arising in the late twentieth century, sought to destabilize this assumption of essences. The critique of essentialism challenges notions of theory focused on "identifying fundamental determinants, 'underlying' structures and mechanisms, or necessary relations" (Graham 53). Many social theorists have charged essentialism with complicity in a reductionist, biological determinism.

Given this critique of essentialism, many feminist scholars began marking a distinction between sex, as the biological difference between males and females, and gender, the social construction of men and women's social roles. However, even this distinction preserves a notion of essence challenged by later feminist thinkers. For example, Monique Wittig (1992) argues that even biological sex is not an essence, and that the body's physiology is "caught up" in processes of social construction. The fact that differences of the body are referenced by these systems (i.e., these systems take up the body in the mobilization of power) makes those differences appear all the more essential. As Stuart Hall (1996) reminds us in the context of race,

> We are readers of race, that is what we are doing, we are readers of social difference. And the body, hair, which you know is cited as if, this is what terminates the argument [...] Well, that very obviousness, the very obviousness of the visibility of race is what persuades me that it functions because it is signifying something; it is a text, which we can read.

Race is not a fixed biological fact; it is something that is read on the body and culturally interpreted. It is not a truth; it is a construct. Questioning notions of Truth, reality, and Western epistemology, critiques of essentialism have opened a terrain of inquiry broadly known as constructivism. Constructivism highlights social and historical change. Constructivists argue not that there is no material world out there, with differences between people—but that the meanings attached to those differences are made in social and cultural practice and change over time. Things do not already contain meanings inside of them; we *make meaning of* things.

A critique of essentialism must be balanced with an understanding of the necessity of collective identity for marginalized groups. To note the limitations of essentialism is not to do away with group identity. Postmodernist and poststructuralist thought sometimes falls to this unfortunate tendency, as bell hooks (1990) explains,

> The postmodern critique of "identity," though relevant for renewed black liberation struggle, is often posed in ways that are problematic. Given a pervasive politic of white supremacy which seeks to prevent the formation of radical black subjectivity, we cannot cavalierly dismiss a concern with identity politics. Any critic exploring the radical potential of postmodernism as it relates to racial difference and racial domination would need to consider the implications of a critique of identity for oppressed groups. Many of us are struggling to find new strategies of resistance. (7)

Group identity has been an important space for social and political mobilization, and certain essentialist ideas have been used strategically in this. "Strategic essentialism" is a term and concept attributed to Gayatri Chakravorty Spivak. In an interview with Elizabeth Grosz, Spivak described strategic essentialism as a tactic "which simultaneously recognizes the impossibility of any essentialism and the necessity of some kind of essentialism for the sake of political action" (qtd. in Buchanan). Spivak has critiqued the way "strategic essentialism" has been taken up by theorists and has subsequently elected to not use the term (see 1993 interview with Sara Danius and Stefan Jonsson in the journal *boundary 2*). Nonetheless, strategic essentialism remains a political tool: Examples of strategic essentialism may function to create visibility and the grounds of collective action.

As it can be a tool for political action, essentialism can also serve to exclude and undermine collective liberation. In her book *The Boundaries of Blackness: AIDS and the Breakdown of Black Politics*, Cathy Cohen shows how narrow definitions of Blackness, which exclude LGBT folks and sex workers within Black communities, hamper our political responses in the face of HIV. The challenge for social movements is to explore ways of building community that both offer space for collective identity, without essentializing the group, thus erasing difference. Our differences are usually our greatest strength.

The implications of a critique of essentialism for creative writers are far ranging. In terms of character development and analysis, we can look at the treatment of difference within a text. Are people figured as static, with fixed characteristics, impervious to time and history? Or are we crafting characters endowed with complex personhood? As Avery Gordon (2004) writes,

Even those living in the most dire circumstances possess a complex and oftentimes contradictory humanity and subjectivity that is never covered by viewing them as victims or as superhuman agents ... Complex personhood means that all people, albeit in specific forms, are beset by contradiction, remember and forget, and recognize and misrecognize themselves and others. Complex personhood means that people suffer graciously and selfishly too, get stuck in what symptomizes their troubles and also transform themselves. (100)

Gender

The keyword gender has been the subject of intense scrutiny over
the past century. It usually denotes historical, cultural, and political
distinctions made between people, grouped into the categories of men
and women, and the gendering of social phenomena through notions
of masculine and feminine. During second-wave feminism, people
began to separate the notions of sex and gender in order to critique
the way that essentialist understandings of sex and sexual difference
assume that the meanings attached to womanhood are the result of
women's physiology. Thus, you encounter concepts like gender roles
which name the social meanings made of physical difference. In
making this distinction, feminist theorists were combatting rampant
biological determinism which rendered patriarchal social relations
inevitable and impervious to political struggle.

Feminist theorists have demonstrated the centrality of gender
as an organizing category for social life. Gender permeates social
interactions and institutions on such a scale that it is part of our
common sense.

In the 1990s, poststructural scholar, Judith Butler radically
reshaped our thinking about gender, emphasizing its performative

dimensions, that it is something we *do*. She theorized gender as a tenuously constituted identity, a "stylized repetition of acts" that resulted in an illusion, the idea of a coherent gendered self. It is worth quoting Butler (1988) at length here:

> To have Become a woman, to compel the body to conform to an historical idea of 'woman,' to induce the body to become a cultural sign, to materialize oneself in obedience to an historically delimited possibility, and to do this as a sustained and repeated corporeal project ... as a strategy of survival, gender is a performance with clearly punitive consequences. Discrete genders are part of what 'humanizes' individuals within contemporary culture; indeed, those who fail to do their gender right are regularly punished. Because there is neither an 'essence' that gender expresses or externalizes nor an objective ideal to which gender aspires; because gender is not a fact, the various acts of gender creates the idea of gender, and without those acts, there would be no gender at all. Gender is, thus, a construction that regularly conceals its genesis. The tacit collective agreement to perform, produce, and sustain discrete and polar genders as cultural fictions is obscured by the credibility of its own production. The authors of gender become entranced by their own fictions whereby the construction compels one's belief in its necessity and naturalness. (522)

Butler's introduction of the notion of gender performativity inaugurated a new era in feminist theory. Butler highlighted the punitive enforcement of gender and the centrality of gender to our notion of the human. She also opened up questions about how gender could be subverted and troubled.

The instability of gender as a foundational concept has been both daunting and productive for feminist theorizing. If there is no ontological unity to the category "woman," how does one go about inaugurating social movements capable of liberating people from patriarchal oppression? Poststructural feminists have argued for a kind of groundless politics, accepting the plurality and instability of meanings. Defining poststructuralism in their volume, *Feminists Theorize the Political* (1992), Judith Butler and Joan Scott write that poststructuralism "is not, strictly speaking, a position, but rather a critical interrogation of the exclusionary operations by which positions are established" (xiv). Scholars have suggested that the category of "woman" is a political tool, which we might strategically take up to advance feminist politics. Joan Scott's (1988) definition of gender is useful, resting on two central propositions: that "gender is a constitutive element of social relationships based on perceived differences between the sexes, and gender is a primary way of signifying relationships of power" (42).

Too often when people say they want to analyze gender, what they mean is that they would like to turn attention on women or point out how a seemingly gender neutral text is, in fact, centered on men. However studying gender is not simply studying women. There is an increasing focus on trans-identities. There is also a large body of work that theorizes masculinity. Joan Acker argues that capitalism as a social project is dependent on particular notions of masculinity. She suggests that there are always multiple "ways of being a man" in a given society, thus we should really talk about masculinities, plural. Taking an intersectional approach invites us to see that race and class inflect the "gender order," to use Raewyn W. Connell's term, and we need to analyze a range of hegemonic (dominant) masculinities and marginalized masculinities. Not all men benefit in the same ways from the dominance conferred on some forms of masculinity.

These feminist interventions into our analysis of gender can help us to build liberatory workshop spaces. Our cultural ideas about writers, often figured as solitary vanguards, are profoundly gendered. This was highlighted with the rise of the popular hashtag #ThingsOnlyWomenWritersHear. In 2017, acclaimed writer Joanne Harris tweeted, "I don't know of any male writer who has been criticized for neglecting his family life, or told he's being selfish for wanting to write … However, I've heard many women writers criticized for the same thing, or being asked how they 'juggle' their writing time and their family" (qtd. in Trautwein 2017).

These constraints and expectations arise from stereotypes and controlling images associated with gender roles. The effects of these stereotypes have profound effects, creating disparities in the publishing industry that have been documented by organizations such as VIDA: Women in Literary Arts. VIDA provides numerical data that illustrates the underrepresentation of women and gender minorities as contributors to major print publications. Any attempt to collect data about gender must be mindful of this complexity of gender identities, including trans and gender nonconforming identities.

Giving full consideration to the complexity of identity is essential in creative writing, as we invoke gender. The tendency to pigeonhole Susan Jane Bigelow describes in an online article titled "A Trans Author on Writing a Trans Character": Speaking of writing the 2010 book *Sky Ranger*, Bigelow remembers thinking, *"Is this going to get me labeled as 'that trans author, you know, the one who only writes about trans people'?"* Bigelow is identifying several problematic assumptions here: the assumption that writers of one minoritized identity write only for people who share that identity; the assumption that only those who have a particular identity will read about it; the assumption that an identity can be reduced to an easy label, the assumption that the ability to write about characters different from oneself is a privilege reserved for the select few.

This last point—the question of who has the ability to write about whom—requires keeping power disparities in full view. Writers have taken a range of stances on this question. In the science fiction publication *Strange Horizons*, Cheryl Morgan writes, "I reject the idea that trans characters should only be written by trans people because cis folk are bound to get it wrong. While there are some really fine trans writers, there simply aren't enough of us in the world to do what is needed. We have to be part of all fiction, not just fiction that we write ourselves." At the same time, there is concern that those who do not experience the world as a trans person can easily fall back on received ideas that stereotype trans characters as suffering, disturbed, deceptive, obsessed with shocking "reveals," freakish, or who are otherwise represented in reductive ways—as mere symbols, or as having lives defined solely by their trans identity and experience of transphobia. At the same time, erasing one's trans identity also does harm: E.J. Levy's novel *The Cape Doctor* is problematically described as: "about the true story of Dr. James Miranda Barry (1795–1865), a flamboyant, brilliant, nineteenth-century physician who rose to prominence [...and] was accused of a scandalous 'homosexual' romance with Lord Charles Somerset, only to be discovered on his deathbed to have been a woman all along." This description not only reinforces stereotypes of the "flamboyant" homosexual along with a "shocking gender reveal" trope, the book also misgenders its central figure.

The problems of pigeonholing and stereotyping tell us that we all need to be reading the books that challenge us, that give full life to the complexity of identity. We need to be reading books that are written by people who represent a range of life experiences, as identity will always escape definitive or predictive analysis. We need to be continually asking ourselves: Where are my ideas about this character coming from? What is gendered in my piece, and am I engaging gender in a way that inhabits complexity and does not fall back on simplistic notions of biology or a gender binary—that does not conflate sex, sexuality and gender and that works to forward respect and inclusion?

Globalization

Manfred B. Stegner defines the term "globalization" in this way, in *Globalization: A Very Short Introduction*: "'Globalization' has been variously used in both popular and academic literature to describe a process, a condition, a system, a force, and an age" (8).

The term "globalization" took hold in a range of conversations in the 1960s, but it is a process that predates the term—a process occurring because of international media, communication, trade, and other economic and social forces that in some ways "shrink the globe" and make the world's populations understand themselves in relation to each other. The world is interdependent and interrelated. As we share a planetary ecosystem, this interconnectedness has always been a reality, but globalization is a process that highlights this fact. Glocalization—a term popularized by Roland Robertson and Zygmunt Bauman—tells us that the local is shaped by the global, and the global is shaped by the local.

All of these aspects of globalization affect the work we do as writers. We are influenced by the work of writers on continents we may never have the means to visit, reading these works in translation from languages that we may never speak. Book publishers inquire about the international market for our work, and we may consider how our work may be received across cultures, in different locations around the world. Texts are increasingly more accessible in the form of e-books. Publication online, without the intermediary of a publishing house, is now possible, with the potential of reaching a broad, international audience. While it remains the case that many people around the world do not have access to the internet, the world is becoming more connected through technology. Manuel Castells has noted the emergence of a global "network society," which he defines as "a society whose social structure is made up of networks powered by micro-electronics-based information and communications technologies" (3).

It's important to remember in noting these transformations that the experience of globalization varies, and people in different parts of the world are affected differently by globalization. Disparities in ability to influence, control, and access forms of social and economic power remain a reality. This reality counters the notion that globalization is a fundamentally democratizing process. There are myths attached to globalization that take the form of progress narratives: the myth, for example, that globalization is unequivocally good for both the "developed" and "developing" worlds. This notion of development assumes a telos or inevitable future for the world that is aligned with capitalist values (think of the influence of transnational corporations), as it overlooks the ways in which globalization has contributed to climate change, ecological devastation, and social inequities. There is also the myth that globalization means the unfettered and free exchange of ideas and cross-cultural understanding, when globalization often is driven by a xenophobic universalizing of Western values. The myths attached to globalization tend to generate a stereotype of the "Other" who is resistant to the progressive ideals of Western superpowers and in need of reform.

History is embedded in any discussion of globalization, and any discussion of globalization is tied to the legacy and ongoing reality of colonialism. Imperialism remains firmly in place in this period of global transition. As Bret Benjamin notes in *Invested Interests*, the World Bank is a cultural as well as economic institution that has had an influential "role in the postwar transformations of imperial power, including its influence (uneven, though undoubtedly potent) over the shape of a postwar system of internationalism, the emerging nation states from the decolonizing Global South, and the increasingly dominant role played by corporate and financial capital" (xx). The World Bank, Benjamin continues, has had a "prominent role in the debt crisis that ravaged the borrowing nations of the Global South throughout the late 1970s and 1980s [which] threw into high relief the institution's historical role as a neocolonial mechanism for the transfer of wealth from South to North" (136). Taking the global as a frame should prompt us to think about power relations as they exist on a worldwide scale—noting the domination of some countries over others. While sometimes posited as an inevitable and natural phenomenon, globalization has emerged specifically from, and is perpetuated by, economic interests of those with power under capitalism.

What we write is affected by world-shaping economic, social, and political forces that transcend national and geographic boundaries. The global is a frame that writers and readers think through, enabling us to see what we write and read through cross-cultural and comparative lenses. The global also calls us to attend to issues of geography, space, and place—accounting for the ways that national and geographic boundaries are constantly shifting in an era of migration and changing coastlines, now more rapidly shifting with the rise of sea levels.

Globalization offers a frame that transcends the boundaries of the nation-state, as it displaces the nation-state from the focal point of analysis. Globalization is related to the term "transnational." In the terms "transnational" and "transcultural" AnaLouise Keating finds the potential to defy "static notions of cultural purity" (66) and an ethnolinguistic understanding of the nation-state—the myth that nation-states define ethnically and linguistically unified groups of people. The global and the transnational have the potential to trouble these myths of homogeneity.

Transnational and world literature has, in just a short time, become a focal point of English departments. Mads Rosendahl Thomsen, in the book *Mapping World Literature*, points to evidence of this change: "The American Comparative Literature Association's decennial report from 1995 was focused on multiculturalism, but did not mention world literature, whereas world literature is the pivotal concept in the report of 2006." Even as English departments may still offer courses that carry the categories of nations (e.g., US literature, British literature, Haitian literature, etc.), these courses are now more likely to take a global perspective. The creative writing workshop space, too, has the global within it.

Identity

In creative writing, we often talk about identity. We talk about the identity of our characters, or the identity of the speakers in our poems, or one's own identity as a writer. When we talk about identity, we might point to individual characteristics, personality types, and preferences. But identity is about more than a single individual's personality; it is also about historical, social, and political contexts. As Beverly Daniel Tatum writes in "The Complexity of Identity: 'Who am I?,'" "The answer depends in large part on who the world around me says I am" (6).

Tatum quotes Erik Erikson, a key researcher in psychology of identity, who writes that when we deal with identity, we deal with what is "'located' *in the core of the individual* and *yet also in the core of his communal culture*" (qtd. in Tatum 6). We learn about who we are from the people we know, from the strangers we encounter and the responses they have to us, from the representations of ourselves we find in the media and literature we engage. What messages are reflected back to us in these interactions, and how do they inform our identities? How we choose *to identify* is conditioned in part by how we *are identified* in the world. How my body is read by others may come to matter in my own regard for my identity.

We don't choose our identities wholecloth with absolute freedom, although there may be parts of our identities that we can choose and choose how to express. Our identity exists in the complex interplay of our embodiment, our desire, our choice, and our imbrication in social relations.

There are many aspects of identity to consider. Pamela Hays devised the acronym "ADDRESSING" to "summarize nine key cultural influences ... addressed in the multicultural and ethical guidelines of the American Psychological Association, the American Counseling Association, and the National Association of Social Workers" (55). The acronym helps us to think of some of the many axes that may influence and shape identity: **A**ge and generational influences, **D**isability, **R**eligion and spiritual orientation, **E**thnic and racial identity, **S**ocioeconomic status, **S**exual orientation, **I**ndigenous heritage, **N**ational origin, **G**ender. The goal in providing this framework is to help understand multiple aspects and layers of identity in an integrated, but non-homogenizing, way.

Each of the letters in the acronym points to what Tatum calls "categories of 'otherness' commonly experienced in US society" (7). To illustrate what she means by "otherness," Tatum runs an exercise with her students in a psychology class. She asks students to list as many descriptors of their identities as they can in sixty seconds. In running this exercise over several years, Tatum has noticed a telling trend: "Students of color usually mention their racial or ethnic group: for instance, [they write] I am Black, Puerto Rican, Korean American. White students who have grown up in strong ethnic enclaves occasionally mention being Irish or Italian. But in general, White students rarely mention being White" (6–7). Tatum observed a similar pattern with other aspects of identity: "Women usually mention being female, while men don't usually mention their maleness. Jewish students often say they are Jews, while mainline Protestants rarely mention their religious identification" (7). From this exercise, Tatum asks her students to reflect on why some identities are more salient than others, as a way of introducing the concept of privilege.

Each of the "ADDRESSING" categories is also tied to an "ism," or a set of "isms"—forms of discrimination that contribute to systemic oppression (e.g., ageism, ableism, religious oppression, ethnocentrism, classism, heterosexism, xenophobia, and sexism). Tatum notes that "the thread and threat of violence runs through all of the isms" (8–9). These "isms" affect us in many ways—determining who has access to what, who is safe from what, and who can decide on what.

Robin DiAngelo offers the following definition of oppression in the book *What Does It Mean to Be White?*: "To oppress is to hold down—to press—and deny a social group full access to resources in a given society. Oppression describes a set of policies, practices, traditions, norms, definitions, cultural stories, and explanations that function to systematically hold down one social group to the benefit of another social group" (61).

To have an intersectional understanding of identity is not to simply add together the letters of the "ADDRESSING" acronym. Rather, intersectionality teaches us to see the particular intermeshing of aspects of identity for each person and circumstance. "Enmeshment" provides a useful metaphor for thinking about identity. Our identities are enmeshed, as María Lugones explains in *Pilgrimages/Peregrinajes: Theorizing Coalition Against Multiple Oppressions*. Lugones resists the kind of thinking that atomizes or separates categories in order to make something manageable. Lugones challenges us to think about identity and intersectionality in messier terms. When we think of oppressive forces as "unified, fixed, atomistic, bounded … " (231), even when we see them in relation to one another, we don't go far enough. Each oppressive force is changed by its relation to other forms of oppression. The particular forms of discrimination experienced by someone who is Black, a trans-female, and Hindu in the United States will be different from those experienced by someone who is Black, cis-gendered, male, and Christian in the United States. And a simple list of identity categories such as this cannot predict who someone is, or their life story. As Lugones notes, identity is "complex and heterogeneous and each person is multiple, nonfragmented, and embodied" (127). We are not a composite of different identity categories, locked together like puzzle pieces. We are not, Lugones notes, made up of a series of "pure parts"—one part gender and one part race, etc. We are instead layered in a way that is exquisitely unpredictable, even as we are enmeshed in structural relations that are based in identity categories.

To describe this layering of identity, Elba Rosario Sánchez uses a geological metaphor. In the essay "Cartohistografía: Continente de una voz," Sánchez tells us: "Identity … is a continuous progression of layer upon layer of soil, building land plates, washing these away to make room for new ones to be exposed" (49). No layer of soil is entirely pure. Our layers are intermixed, as they are also shifting depending on our circumstances, our time and place.

This rejection of the idea of "pure" notions of identity is also a rejection of essentialism. There is no single essence associated with any particular identity. Identity categories provide us with no fixed one-to-one relationship where being Black means being x, y, or z, or where being female means being x, y, or z. There is no fixed formula that enables us to say "x identity category = x trait or characteristic."

If someone is read as Black in an American context, that does not mean that this person would identify as Black. A person might identify as Haitian, but not identify as Black, for example. Moreover, what "Blackness" is, or how "Blackness" is defined, is debatable, and may be entirely up to an individual.

In 1997, Robert M. Sellers et al. published an important study in the *Journal of Personality and Social Psychology*. Titled "Multidimensional Inventory of Black Identity: A Preliminary Investigation of Reliability and Construct Validity," the study asked participants to rate, on a seven-point Likert scale, their level of agreement with statements like "overall, being Black has very little to do with how I feel about myself" and "in general, being Black is an important part of my self-image." The researchers used a Multidimensional Model of Racial Identity (MMRI) to discern African Americans' beliefs regarding the significance of race in (a) how they define themselves and (b) the qualitative meanings that they ascribe to membership in that racial group. The study's findings demonstrate how "racial identity ... is a multifaceted phenomena" (807) that is in part situationally dependent. Sellers's study offers just one portrait of these many faces of racial identity, and models could also be drawn for gender identity, sexual identity, national identity, class identity, and so on.

How a person regards and performs Blackness is in part contextualized by racism and systemic oppression, but it is not limited to that. Race and other social identities have multiple dimensions that can both culturally rich and affirming, while also impacted by oppression. Tommie Shelby makes this point in the book *We Who Are Dark*:

> From the standpoint of black political solidarity, each should be allowed to interpret 'blackness' however [they] see fit, provided the interpretation does not advocate anything immoral and is consistent with the collective struggle for racial justice. In saying this, I am not suggesting, as some have, that individual blacks should give up their various black identities in favor of an American, a cosmopolitan, or simply a 'human' identity. I see no reason to object to blacks identifying with what they regard as their ethnocultural heritage. What I resist is the tendency that blacks must share a distinctive black identity if they are to be a unified force against racial injustice. (236)

Racial injustice is variably experienced by Black people, but that does not mean Blackness is one thing, Shelby argues. Black identity is radically variable. Identity is not fixed and coherent. However, that does not mean that one's identity can be anything—that identity is entirely "up for grabs," as Kenneth Goldsmith has posited in the book *Uncreative Writing*. Identity is not merely an individual's free choice. Identity is conditioned, even as individuals represent uniquely layered identities and even as individuals perform and interpret their identities in unique ways. To say that identity is conditioned is, in part, to note that "our ability to claim particular self-constructions and to have those self-constructions recognized by others is," Stephanie Kerschbaum explains, "always mediated by the power dynamics influencing an interaction" (10).

Identity exists in a world where forces of oppression are entrenched, with long histories and complex manifestations. We can't simply select, at will, whatever identity we want. And we can't simply choose to be beyond identity, or "post-identity."

In recent years, a certain set of writers have advocated for post-identity aesthetics. It is no coincidence that the valuation of "post-identity" writing comes primarily from white writers. Returning to Tatum's study, described at the beginning of this chapter, we can see that writers who occupy a position of privilege may be less likely to see their identity as salient in the writing and reading of literary texts; for example, white writers may be less likely to see the whiteness of their texts and their aesthetic theories. Whiteness is about more than privilege, but privilege is an important aspect of whiteness. And that privilege may cause white people to fail to see the pervasive reality of identity-based oppressions.

To attempt a "post-identity" position is to risk denying the forms of oppression that condition our existence. Gloria Anzaldúa's words in the introduction to *Making Face, Making Soul* elucidate what is ignored and misunderstood by post-identity aesthetics:

A woman-of-color who writes poetry or paints or dances or makes movies knows there is no escape from race or gender when she is writing or painting. She can't take off her color and sex and leave them at the door of her study or studio. Nor can she leave behind her history. Art is about identity, among other things, and her creativity is political. (xxiv)

In similar terms, Cathy Park Hong notes in "Delusions of Whiteness and the Avant-Garde":

> The avant-garde's "delusion of whiteness" is the luxurious opinion that anyone can be "post-identity" and can casually slip in and out of identities like a video game avatar, when there are those who are consistently harassed, surveilled, profiled, or deported for whom they are. But perhaps that is why historically the minority poets' entrance into the avant-garde's arcane little clubs has so often been occluded. We can never laugh it off, take it all in as one sick joke, and truly escape the taint of subjectivity and history. But even in their best efforts in erasure, in complete transcription, in total paratactic scrambling, there is always a subject—and beyond that, the specter of the author's visage—and that specter is never, no matter how vigorous the erasure, raceless.

When—within predominantly white, or white-centered, conversations—purportedly "universal" aesthetic forms are elevated over "cultural texts," we can see the racism and bias of those who occupy a centered position in the field. As Cathy Park Hong notes, constructs of the "universal"—the text that transcends or escapes identity—ultimately amount to a reinforcement of white supremacy.

Dorothy Wang has documented the white-centering of poetry studies in her book *Thinking Its Presence*. Wang critiques the biases at work in the notion that

> because of 'politically correct' cultural-studies-ish pressures in the academy ... worthy, major, and beloved works of literature—whose merits are "purely literary"—are being squeezed out of the

curriculum by inferior works penned by minority writers, whose representation in the curriculum is solely the result of affirmative action or racial quotas or because their writings have passed an ideological litmus test, not literary merit. (157)

Those who uphold the view that is summarized by Wang here expose their bias and racism. We might call this notion a kind of "center-stealing," where those who occupy a privileged position object to the inclusion of those who are "othered." "Center-stealing" refers to the feeling that even slight attention to the "othered" is taking something away from those who historically have been centered. Hence the feeling that the centered works are supposedly being "squeezed out of the curriculum." Wang calls us to think critically about the regimes of value that operate in literary studies to tell us what counts as superior or inferior. These regimes of value construct what counts as "purely literary"; within this construct, the "literary" gets constructed over and against "racialized" literatures, while the whiteness of the narrowly (and problematically) defined "literary" remains naturalized and invisible.

As writers like Wang show us, it is necessary to continue to develop a robust language for naming the complexities of identity within systems of oppression. The work of developing a language that is up to the task of describing identity is a project that will never be complete.

Indigenous

There is no possibility of summatively defining what it means to be Indigenous, or what Indigenous literature includes. As Mareike Neuhaus reminds us, "there are as many Indigenous literatures as there are Indigenous nations" and Indigenous peoples, and "there are also as many Indigenous poetics as there are Indigenous literatures" (2). To attempt to define "Indigenous" is to risk reducing the complexity of the thousands of diverse peoples that identify as Indigenous. As is our goal with all of the entries in the book, our intention here is to invite conversation; it is not to offer the final word on any particular term.

Indigeneity is a category for understanding identity that is distinct from, though related to, race and ethnicity. We chose the term "Indigenous" as the heading for this chapter, rather than "native" or "aboriginal," not because it is the "correct" term to use when discussing tribal communities, but because it is a term that can be regarded as inclusive of many Aboriginal groups in an international or global context. Indeed, the term came into broader usage in the 1970s, during a time of Indigenous coalition-building, which included the 1977 Conference on Discrimination against Indigenous Populations in the Americas.

Indigenous literatures have been misunderstood in Westernized and predominantly white spaces, including the commercialized literary publishing industry and academia. For example, as Neal McLeod writes in the introduction to the collection *Indigenous Poetics in Canada*, "There has been a past tendency in the Anglo-môniyâw publishing world to not consider Indigenous poetry as 'poetry' or to see Indigenous literatures as not meeting their expectations of what poetry is supposed to be" (4). McLeod continues, "Indigenous peoples had poetics long before môniyâwak and English departments existed in our territories" (4), yet this is often overlooked in predominantly white institutions, which are more likely to offer multiple courses that include syllabi composed primarily of white and non-Indigenous authors. This orientation in English studies may perpetuate misunderstanding of Indigenous literatures when they are studied in these spaces: As McLeod writes, "I think that Anglo-môniyâw editors sometimes miss the point of Indigenous poetry—for example, its rhythms and movement through our respective languages, the meaning and significance of Indigenous words, our poetic humour, and the societal context from which our words are derived" (4).

Indigenous literatures cannot be summarized as one entity, but many Indigenous literatures involve what Neuhaus calls the "interarticulation of language, history, ceremony, and land" (4). "Maintaining the balance of these interrelated parts of being," Neuhaus continues, "requires constant care and nurturing" (5).

Storytelling practices are ranging. Some stories are told collectively and in relation to the land. Every being and part of place and community—the valley, the rock, the young people, the elders—may hold part of the story. Storytelling, for some communities, has had an important role in the keeping of knowledge. Story may be how cultural practices, language, and understandings are passed on from one generation to the next. Duncan Mercredi recounts in an essay titled "Achimo,"

> We would ... tell our stories and the storytellers would carry these stories back to repeat on their journey home. It was important that these stories be told exactly as they heard them. It was very, very important that they did not digress whatsoever from the way they were told. It had to be very, very clear and precise because once you changed, even slightly, the order of the story, it could affect the whole family and would continue to affect them for years. (18)

To what extent do creative writing classrooms make space for this regard for one another's story? Do we come to the workshop with this attention, holding stories for each other instead of holding forth?

Such questions shed light on the culturally specific formation that is the writing workshop. The ways of conducting a workshop that have become commonplace in university creative writing are specific to the academic setting, particularly in predominantly white institutions.

The logics of colonialism have shaped settler literatures. Indeed, these literatures have helped to sustain settler-colonialism, as they have reinforced what Mark Rifkin calls "settler common sense" in his book of that title. Consider, for example, literary renderings of wilderness that present a sense that it is the divine right and responsibility of the colonial figure to tame and subdue a vast, "empty," and "wild" landscape. Indeed, no landscape is "empty." And the landscapes that have been the objects of settler-colonial attentions have been inhabited and cultivated for centuries before European arrival. Literary archetypes, such as that of wilderness or the frontier, have reinforced settler-colonial logics. Moreover, stereotypes of the Indigenous person who is "stuck in time," emotionless and tragic, are stereotypes that need to be rooted out of settler literatures. Settler writing may exhibit deep ignorance of diverse tribal communities, applying terms (such as "Eskimo") without understanding their cultural significance. It is our responsibility to recognize how these tendencies operate in the texts that we read and write, in order to reveal them as not "givens" in our world, but rather as harmful, imposed ideas used to justify violence and genocide. In doing this work of "unsettling" settler-colonialism, Indigenous literatures invite what Waaseyaa'sin Christine Sy in "Through Iskigamizigan (The Sugar Bush): A Poetics of Decolonization" calls the "act of resistance, reclamation, and continuance" (189).

Indigenous literatures invite readers and listeners to better understand the uniqueness and importance of orality and the necessity of preserving cultural languages that have cultural knowledge embedded within them. Mercredi emphasizes both the importance of oral storytelling and poetry, and the importance of multilingualism. The limitations of translation from voice to page are matched in the limitations of translation from one language to another: " ... when we translate from our Indigenous languages a poem we have written ... " Mercredi writes, "Once we see it in translation, we tell ourselves, that's not what we meant" (21).

Indigenous literatures also invite readers and listeners to think about rightful use. We learn to ask: Is this particular story meant to be told in this season, in this place?

There are many opportunities to read and learn more. Writers can turn to Indigenous-run presses like Theytus, Kegedonce, Pemmican; organizations like the Indigenous Literary Arts Association, Association for Studies in American Indian Literatures, and the Native American Literature Symposium; and journals like *Wicazo Sa*. Many Indigenous scholars and writers agree that the process of decolonization needs story and poetry, to speak back to the literary legacy of settler-colonialism.

Intersectionality

In the second decade of the twenty-first century, intersectionality is a concept which has entered mainstream discourse. Despite the newness of the concept for some audiences, this term and the meanings it connotes have been influential in shaping feminist and anti-racist politics for several decades. Intersectionality is a concept which comes out of women of color feminisms, specifically Black feminist thought. It names the way that systems of oppression (white supremacy, gendered relations of ruling, heteronormativity) buttress one another or work together (Lorde 1984; hooks 1989; Crenshaw 1991; Combahee River Collective 1995). Patricia Hill Collins uses the language of systems which "find meaning in and through one another" to describe this unique relationship.

In "Demarginalizing the Intersection of Race and Sex: A Black Feminist Critique of Antidiscrimination Doctrine, Feminist Theory and Antiracist Politics" and her now classic paper, "Mapping the Margins: Intersectionality, Identity Politics, and Violence against Women of Color," Kimberlé Crenshaw introduced the concept of "intersectionality." In so doing, Crenshaw fundamentally altered the landscape of feminist theory. Intersectionality "offers a way of mediating the tension between assertions of multiple identity and the ongoing necessity of group politics" (18). In "Mapping the Margins … " Crenshaw distinguishes between three types of intersectionality: structural, political, and representational. In this way, Crenshaw uses intersectionality to refer respectively to (1) the structural conditions of gendered racism as they impact women of color's experiences of violence, (2) the way that both feminist and anti-racist politics elide the issue of violence against women of color because of their singular focus on either gender or race; this political marginalization results in a "location that resists telling" for women of color, and (3) the representation of women of color in popular culture that elides their social location and the violence they face (1242).

Even earlier than Crenshaw's work, other Black feminists were exploring this concept using other language. For example, the now-famous 1977 "A Black Feminist Statement" by the Combahee River Collective argued that "we are actively committed to struggling against racial, sexual, heterosexual, and class oppression and see as our particular task the development of integrated analysis and practice based upon the fact that the major systems of oppression of interlocking" (qtd. in McCann and Kim 2010, 106). The collective's language here is instructive. "The fact that these systems are interlocking" is a condition of their existence; it names how race, class, gender, and sexuality function in their lives. But intersectionality here is also about the "development of integrated analysis and practice." Based on their social location, something can be said about how power moves, and they use this location as a basis for developing theory and practice. Intersectionality is thus "an account of power" (Cooper 386).

At the beginning of the twenty-first century, a number of criticisms have begun to be leveled at intersectionality. As Brittney Cooper, author of *Beyond Respectability: The Intellectual Thought of Race Women* (2016), argues:

> After more than a quarter century of traversing feminist academic terrain, there is an increasing concern that intersectionality has outlived its analytic usefulness. Some argue, implicitly rather than explicitly, that its overarching investment in speaking about the social conditions of US black women's lives militates against its ability to offer a broadly applicable set of theoretical propositions. Others are disillusioned with intersectionality's inability to fully account for all the exigencies of identity in the face of multiple and proliferating categories of social identity, such as sexuality, nation, religion, age, and ability, in contemporary intersectional discourses. Yet, the political import of paradigms that make the interactive process of social marginalization visible cannot be denied. The institutional transformation of the status of women of color feminisms within the academy is a direct result of the political work that intersectional frames do. Thus, there is a tension about what it might mean to jettison or move *beyond* intersectionality's theoretical concerns without jettisoning a commitment to its social-justice aims. (386–387)

In her book *Terrorist Assemblages: Homonationalism in Queer Times*, Jasbir Puar argues for new modes of identity, based on Gilles Deleuze and Félix Guattari's notion of assemblage. Puar sees an intersectional frame as keeping axes of difference (race, class, gender, etc.) as overly separate and discrete: "As a tool of diversity management and a mantra of liberal multiculturalism, intersectionality colludes with the disciplinary apparatus of the state—census, demography, racial profiling, surveillance—in that 'difference' is encased within a structural container that simply wishes the messiness of identity into a formulaic grid" (212). Puar argues that we should not do away with intersectionality, but argues for a supplement with the notion of assemblage, which avoids stabilizing identity categories. Puar is interested in such a move in order to counter what she sees as a complicity between intersectional analysis and US empire-building. What Puar misses is the necessity of an intersectional frame for combatting state violence within the empire. She confuses naming the way that our bodies are sorted, managed, and made vulnerable to "premature death" with claims for recognition based on that experience (Gilmore 28). Intersectionality is not just a framework for identity but also a critique of power relations.

Patricia Hill Collins and Sirma Bilge theorize intersectionality as both a form of critical inquiry and a form of critical praxis. When people "imagine intersectionality, they tend to imagine one or the other, inquiry or praxis, rather than seeing the interconnections between the two." Intersectionality helps us to notice, name, and act.

The misuses of intersectionality include confusing it with a simple concept of interrelatedness. Gloria Anzaldúa writes in the introduction to *Making Face, Making Soul*:

Often white feminists want to minimize racial difference by taking comfort in the fact that we are all women and/or lesbians and suffer similar sexual-gender oppressions. They are usually annoyed with the actuality (though not the concept) of "differences," want to blur racial difference, want to smooth things out—they seem to want a complete, totalizing identity. Yet in their eager attempt to highlight similarities, they create or accentuate 'other' differences … These unacknowledged or unarticulated differences further widen the gap between white and colored. (xxi)

It is important that intersectionality not be used to simply erase difference and complexity. We are interconnected but we are not all the same. Our experiences are disparately conditioned. Intersectionality provides a way of naming these disparities. A wide variety of intellectual and political projects have come under the umbrella of intersectionality and this is by no means a settled framework.

Language

Creative writers work with language. Language is the material of writing; it's what we work with, as a potter works with clay. Through language, writers make meaning. Our languages construct our realities; they construct our worlds—both on and off the page.

There are over 7,000 languages in the world. Each individual may have varying levels of access and exposure to a subset of these languages. At least 60 of the more than 7,000 languages have over ten million users. At the same time, we may employ languages and codes that are not formally recognized in statistics like this. We mix languages, create hybrid languages, invent specialized lexicons for specific situations (think of the language use associated with certain videogames, for example). All languages—whether formally classified or not—are constantly changing and evolving. For this reason, they've often been referred to as "living"—living languages.

Language is inherently social. Indeed, the annually published *Ethnologue: Languages of the World* defines a language as that which has "mutual intelligibility." We adopt languages because they are shared— languages allow for shared meaning. They allow for "communing" and the "common"—words that share a root with the word *communication*.

In turn, language is tied to the complexity of belonging. Use of a particular language may be one way of demonstrating that one is part of a group, although familiarity with a group's language is not sufficient for gaining entrance into that group.

Because language is social, it is also tied to power relations. Linguistic politics play out in every space. Think about the spaces that you move between (classrooms, residence halls, public spaces, domestic spaces, etc.): which languages are valued in each space? Perhaps the languages that you use at home are different from the ones you use on campus.

We see the relationship between language and power when we think about how language gets "corrected." Think about the phrases you've heard used to evaluate someone's language: perhaps you've heard the sentence "this writing needs to be 'cleaned up.'" Think about the word-choice in this phrase. Why do we talk about language as "clean" or not "clean"? Does this sentence imply that some writing (and, by implication, some *writers*) is, or are, "unclean"—a word that might be associated with immorality, filth, etc.? What other words do we use to talk about writing and language use: for example, "poor," "wrong," "deficient," etc.? Do these words assume a link between "good speech" and "good character"?

"Linguistic terrorism" is a term that Gloria Anzaldúa has written about in the well-known essay "How to Tame a Wild Tongue," which is part of the landmark book *Borderlands/La Frontera*. Thinking of the colonial context in which colonized subjects have been punished and harmed for speaking their native tongue, Anzaldúa illustrates the ways in which cultural erasure and dehumanization happen through linguistic terrorism. Anzaldúa explains linguistic terrorism in this way: "If a person … has a low estimation of my native tongue, she also has a low estimation of me" (58). She continues,

> Ethnic identity is twin skin to linguistic identity—I am my language. [...] Until I am free to write bilingually and to switch codes without having always to translate, while I still have to speak English or Spanish when I would rather speak Spanglish, and as long as I have to accommodate the English speakers rather than having them accommodate me, my tongue will be illegitimate. (59)

As Anzaldúa illustrates, some codes count as legitimate and "right," while others are disparaged or demeaned. There are languages that are tied to power and that carry cultural capital in institutionalized spaces; "there are codes or rules for participating in power; that is, there is a 'culture of power'" that is tied to language (24), writes education theorist Lisa Delpit in the book *Other People's Children*. Delpit argues that students in school should be explicitly taught to "code-switch"— or to move between the codes associated with the culture of power and the codes that may be used in students' home communities. Delpit explains, "If you are not a participant in the culture of power, being told explicitly the rules of that culture makes acquiring power easier" (24). By teaching multiple codes, and giving equal attention and legitimacy to each, students can be better equipped to navigate the world, and to use the varieties of codes available to them for different purposes.

Many theorists have written in similar terms about the relationship between language and power: How does the relationship between language and power manifest in creative writing? What are the codes of power associated with literature? We can remember that, as Delpit writes, "those with power are frequently least aware of—or least willing to acknowledge—its existence. Those with less power are often most aware of its existence" (24). Given these circumstances, how can we discuss in frank terms the languages of power that might operate in creative writing—while also refusing to uphold "the illusion of a monolingual environment," to use a phrase presented in Janet Neigh's essay "Dreams of Uncommon Languages" from the journal *Feminist Formations*.

Multilingualism characterizes our world. Valuing multilingualism means engaging the multiple languages that shape our existence and the existence of those about whom we write. Valuing multilingualism also means examining the relationship between language and power in discussions about "accented" dialogue and the use of dialect and vernacular in our writing. We do well to treat each dialect as a language in its own right, a language that demands close attention and study. Those who are not adept and fluent users of a particular dialect or vernacular should be sharply aware of the risk of caricaturing a language user.

Writers need to be mindful for the politics of "Standard English" and the colonial history of erasing languages with the forced adoption of a dominant code. Cultural knowledges are embedded in language. Robin Wall Kimmerer's chapter "Learning the Grammar of Animacy" in *Braiding Sweetgrass* emphasizes this point. Kimmerer explicates the environmental knowledges that may be lost if Indigenous languages are not valued and preserved. Kimmerer writes of the Anishinaabe word *puhpohwee*, which roughly translates in English to "the force which causes mushrooms to push up from the earth overnight." This word contains within it an ability to see something—the animacy of the mushroom in its interaction with the earth—that might be lost if we did not have the word. Cultural knowledges are embedded in languages: in the denotative meanings of words and in the structures of their grammars. Creative writers who work in translation know this. The work of translation may support the preservation and valuing of the full range of human languages.

The fact that cultural knowledges and assumptions are embedded in language also means something for dominant discourses. As Toni Morrison describes in *Playing in the Dark: Whiteness and the Literary Imagination*, "I am a black writer struggling with and through a language that can powerfully evoke and enforce hidden signs of racial superiority, cultural hegemony, and dismissive 'othering' of people and language" (x). She continues, "The kind of work I have always wanted to do requires me to learn how to maneuver ways to free up the language from its sometimes sinister, frequently lazy, almost always predictable employment of racially informed and determined chains" (xi). This is the work of a creative writer. We learn to examine our language with an ever-broadening knowledge of what is at stake in our choices.

Minoritized

People of color may sometimes be referred to as "minorities," even in spaces and on occasions where the number of people of color actually makes up a numerical majority. We can see that the noun "minority," when used to label a group of people, becomes problematic. We are not naming population size; we are naming something else.

The root word "minor" can mean "of lesser importance or significance." There is thus a risk in referring to people groups as "minorities." This word can serve to reinforce a "lesser" status, assigning it as a characteristic of a people group, rather than a characteristic of the system that makes certain people lesser. When we use a cognate of the word "minor," we should use it to point to structural relations that *minoritize* people—that prejudicially and wrongfully consider some to be "lesser than." The verb *minoritize* helps us to see that this is something that is *actively done to* a group of people; it is not what or who they *are*.

As Abdul JanMohamed and David Lloyd write in *The Nature and Context of Minority Discourse*, to be

minor is not a question of essence (as the stereotypes of minorities in dominant ideology would want us to believe), but a question of position: a subject position that in the final analysis can be defined only in 'political' terms—that is, in terms of the effects of economic exploitation, political disenfranchisement, social manipulation, and ideological domination on the cultural formation of minority subjects and discourses. (7)

In other words, it is not that one is a "minority" in having an identity that is "other" to a "majority" identity. It is instead that some are "minoritized" through systems of exploitation, disenfranchisement, and domination. When we use "minority" as a noun, we should be careful to specify that we are talking about a *numerical* minority so as to invoke the specific meaning of "minority" we intend, and not the additional definitions and connotations that come with this term.

The paired terms "majoritized versus minoritized" present one way of describing the structural forces that create disparities and inequalities. You may be familiar with some other paired terms such as "center versus margin." Intersectional scholars have offered a "critique of the margin-center understanding of power," as Doris Sommer notes (58), demonstrating that there is no single oppressor that oppresses all peoples on all sides. Rather oppressions are structural, multi-dimensional, and interconnected. There is also the risk that these paired terms will come to reinforce the very relations that they were created to name. To name a community as "peripheral" or "marginal" is to risk reinforcing that status.

To escape this risk, writers have adopted several strategies. Doris Sommer in the book *Proceed with Caution, When Engaged by Minority Writing in the Americas* (1999) shows how some texts foreground their "minoritized" status by mocking majoritized readers' "assumption that they can know a text through their interpretive reading strategies."

Those who conceive of themselves as occupying a "majority" position fantasize their worldview to be "standard" or "universal" or "the way things are" for all. Sommer is interested in the ways that "minority" writing confronts this notion by marking cultural difference and refusing to be read as universally relatable, universally understandable. These texts offer no "coauthorship" (xiii) or sense from the reader that they have come to know the text, and therefore have shared in its writing. These texts work against the common reader-response practice where a reader incorporates the text in their own experience without first interrogating positionality and the power relations that shape identity. Sommer likens these mainstream reader-response approaches to that of a Western ethnographer who feels entitled to know the "other" and to bring the "other" into the ethnographer's own paradigm. Sommer's analysis of minority writing focuses on texts that do not invite this kind of reading. Instead, minority writing escapes or subverts the reader's demand to know; these texts employ strategies such as circumlocutions, deferred translation, withheld information, secrets, absence of intimate details, refusal to confess, or a kind of unstinting availability that produces only boredom (akin to the "featherbed resistance" that Zora Neale Hurston described). With such strategies, these texts "cripple [the reader's] authority by refusing to submit to it" (10).

In this argument, Sommer borrows from Norma Klahn, in utilizing the term "particularist literature" as that which mocks the desire for the "universal." Norma Klahn proposes a "particularist" reading instead of a "universalist" one that would neither maintain the "other" as an essentialized exotic other, nor assimilate the "other" to self. "Particularist" literature carves out a space for that which is "minoritized"—claiming and protecting this "minor" space as sovereign and untouchable by those who would utilize a majority framework for understanding.

Theorists like Doris Sommer and Norma Klahn evaluate the ways that a "minoritized" status can be used creatively by those who struggle against and resist dominating forces. This orientation is in some ways different from that of Gilles Deleuze and Félix Guattari who pose a "minor" literature as that which "deterrioritalizes" with an immediate social and political function. Deleuze and Guattari value minor literature for its capacities to destabilize existing regimes of meaning and to throw off existing forms of domination, which they tie to the establishing of one's own territory.

However, theorists such as Rafael Pérez-Torres are critical of Deleuze and Guattari's theory of minor literature. In *Movements in Chicano Poetry: Against Myths, Against Margins*, Pérez-Torres identifies how the strategies represented by Deleuze and Guattari "simply appropriate and remarginalize the oppressed subjects that form the sociohistorical margin" (224). "The 'minor' as a key struck by Deleuze and Guattari cannot exist without the 'minority' that lives and breathes the deterritorializations" (224), Pérez-Torres notes, and he shows how this tendency in Deleuze and Guattari is common to white poststructuralist thought. Pérez-Torres notes, "much of poststructural thought has cast the marginalized further into the margins through dehistoricized celebration and disempowering reification" (225) of a minoritized status. Celebrating being "minoritized" as that which we should seek is very different from recognizing and honoring the creativity of those who have been minoritized; the first perspective (i.e., the "minoritized" experience as that which we should seek) assumes a position of privilege, while the second perspective (i.e., honoring the creativity of those who have been minoritized) works to dismantle the systems that create the effect of minoritization. The first perspective assumes that marginality is an inherently liberating force, while the second perspective knows differently: it knows the minoritized status to be ambivalent and complicated and full of struggle. George Yúdice in "Marginality and the Ethics of Survival," an article published in *Social Text* in 1989, is another important source that makes the case against the oversimplified idealization of marginality as something to be sought.

In creative writing craft textbooks, one often finds the "renegade" or "outlaw" writer presented as an ideal. Those writers who do not conform, who do things their own way, are celebrated for their unique genius. At first glance, it might seem that these "outlaw" writers are minoritized, existing outside a "mainstream." But the identity of the "outlaw" writer is imagined as an identity that one can *choose*. Indeed craft texts encourage young or novice writers to make that choice. And this "outlaw" status does not come with any of the conditions experienced by those who become penalized by the criminal justice system, a system that disproportionately imprisons people of color. The celebration of the "outlaw" status is one example of how privilege operates in creative writing. There is a world of difference between the success of an "insider" figure who decides to construct an "outsider" status, and the challenge that writers of color face in an industry that demonstrably privileges the writing of male and white writers (see the statistics provided by the VIDA Count and other statistical analyses of diversity in publishing for evidence of this). We do well to keep this in mind as we encounter constructions of "insider-outsider" figures in creative writing.

Multiculturalism

If "multiculturalism" is another term for valuing diversity and cultural pluralism, the term may at first seem to be an uncomplicated idea—something that we should desire. But the use of this term has a vexed and complex history.

At its best, multiculturalism enables us to dismantle an assumption of a monocultural identity; it helps us to see our own cultural assumptions more clearly and recognize them as contingent and as part of a pluralistic world. And it helps to identify and change uneven power relations, which cause some cultural ideas to become normative and some cultural players to become dominant. At its best, in other words, multiculturalism would allow us to dismantle what María Lugones, in an essay titled "Hablando cara a cara/Speaking Face to Face," calls "the ideology of the ethnocentric racial state which privileges the dominant culture as the only culture to 'see with'" (51).

However, multiculturalism may end up reinforcing this very idea of dominant culture. The ideology that privileges one's way of seeing may show up cloaked in an idea of "melting-pot multiculturalism." The melting-pot is about assimilation, neutralization, and obliteration of distinct cultures in the name of "valorizations of melting-pot multiculturalism's sameness," to use AnaLouise Keating's words in the book *Transformation Now!* (68).

When it escapes this melting-pot tendency, multiculturalism, as a concept, can be useful in disrupting the naturalization of white culture as "no culture"—the tendency to see white and dominant cultures as invisible and normative and universal. Multiculturalism helps us to see that there are cultural assumptions embedded in everything we write, and everything we do in creative writing.

Consider, for example, the value that is often placed on print publication in creative writing. Many cultures value orality and the ephemeral in-the-moment coming-into-being of creation. Creation is collective, and it is cooperative with the specificity of each place. We might generate a story together, and this rock and that tree have a role in creating the story. Publishing in print is not a value here. It would be difficult, if not impossible, to translate this form of collective-creation-with-place to a static page. Therefore, we see that the single author at work in solitude on a page is a culturally specific idea, and the value placed on the solitary reader's response to a text is likewise culturally specific.

To embrace multiculturalism is to expose the cultural specificity and contingency of each practice, seeking to invite and value a multitude of ways of knowing, ways of doing, ways of being. This type of multiculturalism requires considerable effort. It thwarts the systems that have held to a narrow set of practices, a set of practices that privilege some over others.

This vision of multiculturalism is rarely realized. Yet the word "multiculturalism" circulates regularly and widely. Think of the "diversity statement" that is regularly included in organization's websites, marketing materials, and HR documents. This boilerplate diversity statement says that multiculturalism is an institutional value. Sara Ahmed argues in her book titled *On Being Included* that institutional diversity statements fleetingly *perform* a value of diversity; they do not report a reality. What these diversity statements say may have little to do with an institution's realized level of equity and inclusion. For example, a university may have a clear diversity statement and at the same time have only (or almost exclusively) white, heterosexual, cis-gendered males in its leadership positions. "Being judged to have written an exemplary race equality policy is quickly translated into being good at race equality," Ahmed notes. "Such a translation works to conceal the very inequalities the documents were written to reveal" (100).

Like the "diversity statement" that Ahmed writes about, the term "multiculturalism" may likewise occlude actual structural inequity. While institutional value statements might attract a more diverse student body, there is a risk that this diversity will be treated as a kind of capital—something to be collected and profited from. Think about the images that you see on institutional marketing materials. Often you'll find a diverse set of students and faculty in every picture. While this may be a well-intentioned attempt to cultivate a sense of belonging among prospective and current students, there is also the risk that institutions will orient toward diverse peoples "as if they are raw materials that can enhance the educational products they are 'selling'" (Kerschbaum 37).

When a discussion of diversity is uncoupled from analysis of inequity, these risks are at the fore. Lacking an analysis of power, multiculturalism can easily become what Trinh Minh-ha describes in *When the Moon Waxes Red: Representation, Gender, and Cultural Politics* as "the juxtaposition of several cultures whose frontiers remain intact" (232, quoted in Keating 64). Being presented with the benign coexistence of different peoples and different cultural traditions may cause us to lose sight of the continued histories of colonialism that contribute to structural inequity. That legacy of colonialism has been about the profiting of one culture off another, as the culture in power has sought the erasure and eradication of others.

The idea of multiculturalism as "benign coexistence" has an additional problem: Not only does this idea of multiculturalism lack an understanding of power differentials, it also can tend to compartmentalize people. What AnaLouise Keating calls "separatist multiculturalism" fixes people's identities into neat categories, taxonomizing different cultures from a particular perspective. This can lead to tokenism—a kind of perfunctory performance of multiculturalism. Tokenism happens when a symbolic representative from each of a selected set of racial, ethnic, or other identity categories is included, while what has historically been dominant remains in a dominant position. Tokenism also may make one person a "representative of" all peoples of a particular identity category.

In its tokenism, "separatist multiculturalism" tends to be fundamentally essentializing, and obsessed with "cultural authenticity." This results in what is often referred to as "pigeonholing" (Selasi 2015). Writers are pigeonholed when they are expected to deliver on a dominant idea of what they are.

How do we escape these problematic tokenizing and assimilationist tendencies of multiculturalism? Our response can be one of self-reflection and humility. The idea of "cultural humility" must be central to multiculturalism, if we are to avoid the pitfalls described here. Summarizing Tervalon & Murray-Garcia's 1998 essay "Cultural Humility Versus Cultural Competence," Miguel E. Gallardo writes in the edited collection *Developing Cultural Humility: Embracing Race, Privilege, and Power* (2014): "Cultural humility has been defined as a lifelong process of self-reflection, self-critique, continual assessment of power imbalances, and the development of mutually respectful relationships and partnerships." Cultural humility means researching one's own identities and the histories that inform them, excavating privilege, and identifying responsibilities in a world that is characterized by inequity.

In the same collection, Joseph G. Ponterotto explains, in an essay titled "Finding My Cultural Selves," that "multicultural awareness is an evolving and ongoing process." It means asking oneself: "What are my cultural blind spots now? In what areas of race and culture do I lack insight and awareness at this time? Am I being culturally insensitive in my interactions or expectations today?" (40). Ponterotto's essay advocates finding a "multi-paradigmatic" approach to one's work—an ability to shift into multiple perspectives and to see one's work from the vantage point of different histories and legacies, to "move across cultural boundaries" (44), as Eduardo Duran puts it in a response essay.

As writers we have the opportunity to see our cultural identities reflected back to us on the page. This is an occasion to come to better understand oneself in a global context, a context that is characterized by a multitude of cultural perspectives. Culture is a central category for thinking about ourselves and our writing.

National

Have you ever taken a course in "British Literature" or "American Literature"? These course titles tell us something about the relationship between literature and the nation. Why is it common to organize literary curricula based on national boundaries?

Literature produced in, or focused on, a particular country may be a source of national pride. Literature has been used to shore up national borders and to offer members of a nation particular representations of themselves. In other words, literature is a form of nation-building. Indeed, as Kwame Anthony Appiah noted in the 2017 MLA Presidential Address titled "Boundaries of Culture," the term "literature" as we know it was co-emergent with nation; the two were born twins, as it were.

National literature is a space "where meanings may be partial because they are *in media res;* and history may be half-made because it is in the process of being made; and the image of cultural authority may be ambivalent because it is caught, uncertainly, in the act of 'composing' its powerful image," as Homi K. Bhabha notes in the introduction to the anthology *Nation and Narration*. In their partiality, ambivalence, and continual emergence, literatures can serve to contribute to a sense of national identity. Nations are, after all, Benedict Anderson notes, *imagined*. Anderson poses the following definition of a nation: a nation "is an imagined political community— and imagined as both inherently limited and sovereign" (6).

This imagined nation creates notions of what and who is legitimate within national boundaries. Citizenship is about legal status, rights, political participation, and it can be denied on the basis of race, ethnicity, religion, gender, sexuality, or class. An idea of nation is an idea of belonging (sometimes figured by who is legitimized and enfranchised as a "citizen"). We know that belonging is always defined against that which does not belong—what is "othered." Thus, we can see how concepts of nation reinforce social hierarchies. What counts as national literature—and what becomes folded into a dominant idea of a national tradition—is often what serves a dominant group. We see this politics of national belonging manifest in state-initiated censorship of literatures and the exiling of writers from their home countries based on the politics of their writing. Decisions to censor, ban, or exile writers and their writing are based on ideas of the nation—and what counts as legitimate to it.

The construct "nation," as we understand it today, is a fairly recent phenomenon in human history. Nations are not naturally occurring. Nations don't emerge the way coastlines emerge, through geological shifts. National boundaries are drawn and redrawn as political formations, and, as such, nations are fundamentally unstable. The editors of the text *Postcolonial Studies: The Key Concepts* make this point:

As thinkers as early as Renan were aware … the instability of the nation is the inevitable consequence of its nature as a social construction. The myth of nationhood, masked by ideology, perpetuates nationalism, in which specific identities are employed to create exclusive and homogenous conceptions of national traditions. Such signifiers of homogeneity always fail to represent the diversity of the actual 'national' community for which the purport to speak. (167)

Etymologically tied to the word "race," nations are often misconstrued to be "discrete ethnological units unambiguously segmented on the ground, thereby naturalizing them along a spatial axis" (Malkki 26), but in fact they are political formations that cut across ethnicity. We might be asked, "What is your nationality?" Sometimes this question is posed, and the questioner means to ask not the nation you were born in, but the ethnicity you have. Nationality is its own category of identity, and, like other categories of identity, nationality is tied to axes of oppression. It is tied to xenophobia and nativism, with nativism defined here as the privileging of those deemed to be legitimate citizens of a nation over and above those of immigrants.

As a point of clarification, it's important to understand that this form of nativism, despite its name, is not about the interests of Native American or Indigenous peoples. Rather, nativism creates a hierarchy that elevates a particular idea of a citizen of a country, disregarding treaty agreements with, and the sovereignty of, those who are Native or Indigenous to a land. The nationalist ideology of settler-colonialism has been used to justify histories of forced assimilation and genocide— as part of what Glen Sean Coulthard in *Red Skins, White Masks* calls "the entangled relationship among racism, state power, capitalism, and colonial dispossession" (Coulthard 21). In response and in resistance to settler-state nationalism, Indigenous assertions of nationhood emphasize the claim to communal identification and sovereignty.

Settler-state ideas of national boundaries regularly disregard the land rights of Indigenous peoples. The assumed homogeneity of that which lies within national boundaries is a gesture of erasure—covering over the complex and individuated histories of people-groups in a particular locality.

Existing within a nationalist frame, some literatures uphold a national chauvinism that may, for colonial powers, translate into the universalizing of national values. Writers who work in colonized and decolonizing nations, in contrast, may find themselves pigeonholed by critics and readers who expect that their literatures will speak for the nation, or even a whole continent. Aijaz Ahmad cites a *New York Times* review that characterizes Salman Rushdie's *Midnight's Children* as representative of a "Continent finding its voice"—as if one voice and one book can be the voice of a continent.

Exhibiting a similarly reductive tendency, Fredric Jameson's 1986 essay "Third World Literature in the Era of Multinational Capital" posits,

What all third-world cultural productions have in common, what distinguishes them radically from analogous cultural forms in the first world [is that] all third-world texts are necessarily ... allegorical, and in a very specific way: they are to be read as what I will call national allegories, even when, or I should say primarily when, their forms develop out of predominantly western machineries of representation, such as the novel. (67)

Aijaz Ahmad's essay "Jameson's Rhetoric of Otherness and the 'National Allegory'" critiques Jameson's famous claim, noting, first, that "there is no such thing as a 'third-world literature'" (4) and, second, that Jameson's claim unfairly reduces and destines these "third-world" literatures to be only one thing: Jameson's claim "divides the world between those who make history and those who are mere objects of it" (7).

What the idea of "nation" means for literature is a question with a changing set of responses. The reliance on national boundaries to classify and characterize literature is fraught. Many works "do not fit into nationalist paradigms, such as the writing of pan-Native, multinational, and urban authors" (8), Mareike Neuhaus notes in the book *The Decolonizing Poetics of Indigenous Literatures*. The nationalist frame for understanding literature is limited in a world in which "more and more people identify themselves, or are categorized, in reference to deterritorialized 'homelands,' 'cultures,' and 'origins'" (24). Liisa Malkki observes this reality in the essay "National Geographic: The Rooting of Peoples and the Territorialization of National Identity among Scholars and Refugees":

> There has emerged a new awareness of the global social fact that, now more than perhaps ever before, people are chronically mobile and routinely displaced, and invent homes and homelands in the absence of territorial, national bases-not in situ, but through memories of, and claims on, places that they can or will no longer corporeally inhabit. (24)

Concurrently, the shift of power from nation-states to supranational institutions and forces (e.g., NAFTA, IMF, the World Bank, etc.)

creates circumstances in which a transnational understanding of literary production is necessary. Arianna Dagnino in the book *Transcultural Writers and Novels in the Age of Global Mobility* offers terms for understanding literature in the context of "the contemporary social condition/lifestyle emerging from the transnational and deterritorialized patterns produced by global mobility and by the intense digitalization of information and communication technologies." Dagnino writes, "This social condition in its turn may generate flexible decentered identities with specific transcultural attitudes and sensibilities."

National boundaries have been foundational to literary history. At the same time, many value literature for its capacity to cross national boundaries. We might value literature for its capacity to connect to human experience and transcend the particularities of one's own identity and lived reality. As Appiah noted in his 2017 MLA Presidential Address, national "boundaries are at once foreign to and constitutive of literature."

Positionality

Positionality is a critical approach to who you are and where you speak from that also acknowledges power relations. We can find this definition in the word itself. The suffix "ality" is used to refer to a condition or quality of being. So positionality (i.e., "position" + "ality") may be thought of as the *condition of having a specific position in society*. By "position in society," we don't mean to refer to a fixed role; a person's "position" is complex and dynamic. Here "position" refers to what you identify with and what you are identified by. Our bodies are read in the world—in how we are embodied, in how we communicate, in how we inhabit space, in how we practice daily living. These daily, moment-by-moment readings of us shape our experiences.

You may experience certain things because of your positionality. In turn, those experiences shape your way of being and your perspective. While there is no one-to-one relationship between having "x" subject-position and being or knowing "y," your positionality may be related to certain experiences in your life that inform what you know. For example, a white person may be more likely to believe that we live in a "post-racial" world because a white person doesn't experience race-based prejudice in the same way as a person of color.

Your positionality is always present when you are writing. All you've come to know about the world, including your perspective and even your immediate perceptions, is influenced by your positionality. The experiences you've had, the ideas and values that you've been most familiar with, the opportunities and resources you've had access to all shape how you see the world and how you translate that world to the page. All of your experiences are conditioned by sociopolitical dimensions. In other words, positionality is about power. Our experiences take place in a world with embedded histories, a world that is characterized by unequal power relations. Racism, classism, sexism, xenophobia, homophobia, and ableism are just some of the ways of naming the different lines by which structures of unequal power relations are drawn. And these lines of power relations never exist in isolation; these lines traverse each other; they influence each other.

Histories of oppression—including colonialism, forms of dispossession and displacement, structural racism, etc.—have shaped what we've had access to, and what we've had access to shapes our way of perceiving the world. For example, if I am someone who has always had access to farmer's markets, it becomes easier for me to pronounce a judgment that people are "good" or "right" if they make their food purchases at farmer's markets. But one can see that my opinion or judgment here is based on my positionality in the world—having the privilege of knowing what a farmer's market is, living near a farmer's market, feeling comfortable in the spaces where farmer's markets exist.

My access to farmer's markets—and my subsequent knowledge and beliefs about them—may be based on socioeconomic class and may also be conditioned by my race (as farmer's markets may, in subtle or overt ways, perpetuate themselves as predominantly white spaces) and may be conditioned by what my body is capable of doing (moving in narrow aisles, having the use of hands for cash exchange and produce selection, etc.). As this example of the farmer's market shows, my beliefs are likely to be informed by my positionality. If I don't pause to identify how my positionality informs my understanding of the world, I may make assumptions that are unfair, faulty, or exclusionary. We can learn to gain a lens that finds what Gloria Anzaldúa calls our "blankspots"—or the places where we may forget to look or listen, the places that may be blanked out in our minds.

The idea of positionality tells us that our perceptions are specific to our situations: our perceptions are contingent and therefore not universal. Nor are our perceptions inevitable. Our perceptions are not fixed. They're not intractable. We can develop a *lens for our lens*—or a way of seeing what we've been predisposed to see.

Part of this work of developing a "lens for our lens" is learning to be explicit about our positionality, to explicitly identify where we are coming from when we write about a specific topic. We do this with the knowledge that words mean differently depending on who is saying them. When I (Janelle) write about colonialism as a white person living in the United States, for example, I acknowledge that I may not be able to fully unsettle the presumptions of settler-colonialism in my perspective. I acknowledge that I may have unacknowledged "blankspots." I seek the input and insights of other writers on my topic, so that they can help to point to what has been blanked out or omitted in my work, what I have failed to see. This also means learning to pose the questions to oneself: "Which perspectives and identities are centered in my writing, and which are left to the margins? What assumptions am I making, and how can I check these assumptions against others' lived experiences?"

Positionality matters in our citation practices as well. Let's say that I am a white person who is writing a creative nonfiction essay about US National Parks. In this essay, I might uphold an assumption that National Parks are good, and that all people should value them. In my essay, I might reference findings from environmental psychology and histories written primarily by white, middle-class academic researchers. My essay may be persuasive to people who already feel favorably toward US National Parks; however, my essay is limited, and potentially harmful, if it fails to acknowledge that the parks were established by the forcible removal of Indigenous peoples from this land. If I come to acknowledge my positionality and the potential bias that may be present in my perspective, I am more likely to come to question my assumptions and point to the complexity of the issue. I may find more culturally pluralistic ways of writing about the values that I want to explore—the values of connection to the land. I prioritze and honor the learning that has been tied to the landscape in tribal communities for centuries, without making the "moves to innocence" described by Eve Tuck and K. Wayne Yang in the essay "Decolonization Is Not a Metaphor."

In our writing, we can work to move toward cultural pluralism, where multiple perspectives can be brought together. Cultural pluralism may involve asking the people whose lives are most directly affected by your topic to provide feedback and peer collaboration on your projects (although such requests should be carefully and respectfully made, in order to ensure freedom and agency and open dialogue for those who are asked to contribute). It may mean deferring to those who have lived experience with your topic as experts—knowing that their stories do not belong to you. It may mean asking permission. It may mean checking your representations. It may mean immersion, or spending time in a specific locality and observing all one can there, with consent from those with whom you'd wish to collaborate. It may mean reading as much as you can, from as many different perspectives as you can, to gain a fuller and more diverse sense of perspectives on the subject at hand. It may mean acknowledging that your positionality makes it impossible or challenging to do certain things with your work.

With the project that you are working on right now, think about how your positionality has shaped what you're interested in and your approach to your subjects. What in your background has influenced what you care about and why? What stance are you taking on your subject, and how is that stance influenced by where you come from? What do you need to consider as you write about this topic? What potential blankspots might emerge for you in this project? Whose experiences are centered? Whose voices are you citing, and whose voices are you leaving out? What does it mean that you, given your positionality, are the person to write this piece? What do you need to consider about your positionality as you think about how your work will be received by different readers? Keep these questions in mind when you are planning and revising your work.

Power

Ultimately, an intersectional framework pushes us to understand the power relations at work in the creative writing classroom. Max Weber writes that power is "the probability that one actor in a social relationship will be in a position to carry out his own will despite resistance" (53). This is a useful definition. But we also must understand that power relations go beyond an individual person's will. Power relations are patterned or structured in society. Many of the keywords in this book relate to entire systems of power, beyond an individual's will, intention, or personality.

Power relations permeate social life, people's interactions with one another, and the distribution of material and symbolic goods. Patricia Hill Collins and Sirma Bilge (2016) identify four domains of power: the interpersonal, structural, disciplinary, and cultural domains of power relations (7). An intersectional approach to power demonstrates how race, gender, sexuality, disability, age, ethnicity, nation, and religion, among other systems, find meaning in and through one another. They operate across domains. In their *Signs* article "Toward a Field of Intersectionality Studies: Theory, Applications, and Praxis," Cho, Crenshaw, and McCall argue for a notion of intersectionality as an analytic approach which conceives "of categories not as distinct but as always permeated by other categories, fluid and changing, always in the process of creating and being created by dynamics of power" (Cho et al., 795).

But, how does power work? Increasingly, critical scholars and activists are moving to a nuanced and subtle analysis of power relations. Creative writers must aim to do this as well if we are to express the complexities of identity and subjectivity in the world. Using an intersectional perspective requires us to operate with a more complex analytics of power. The work of Michel Foucault marked a decisive rupture in critical inquiry regarding the workings of power. Foucault argued that classical Marxism had too often reduced power to a mechanism of elite economic interests, sharing problematic assumptions with liberal conceptions of political power or the classical juridical theory of power that is epitomized by the philosophers of the eighteenth century. Many Marxist thinkers throughout the twentieth century have tended to adopt a mechanistic conception of power, treating power like a tool or hammer. Think of the phrase, "bringing the hammer down" on someone. Michel Foucault provided us with an important critique of this way of thinking of power.

In the first of his lectures at the Collège de France in the 1975–1976 academic year, Foucault argues that both Marxist and Liberal analyses of power are plagued by an "economism." Liberal theories regard power as a right, which can be possessed like one possesses a commodity (Foucault 1980, 88–89). In this formulation, power is reduced to a kind of economic exchange like the exchange of contracts. Classical Marxist conceptions of power have often shared this economism, and this is Foucault's primary issue in beginning to reformulate a theory of power. Classical Marxism has operated with an analysis, which Foucault terms, the "economic functionality" of power:

> Economic functionality to the extent that the role of power is essentially both to perpetuate the relations of production and to reproduce a class domination that is made possible by the development of the productive forces and the ways they are appropriated. In this case, political power finds its historical raison d'être in the economy. (Foucault 2003, 14)

Foucault sought to develop a way of thinking about power that could go beyond economism to account for the ways in which mechanisms of power transverse the entire social body, including but not limited to the economic. For Foucault, power is fundamentally bound up with knowledge. He often wrote of power-knowledge, refusing to even separate the two terms. Whenever power is being exercised, forms of knowledge are being founded; and conversely, in the assertion of knowledge, power is being exercised. Power relations entail claims about who groups of people are (knowledge of a population), and this power makes it so that some forms of knowledge are made true. Power produces "regimes of truth."

Foucault encourages us to see power in much more subtle terms, as decentralized and permeating social life. As Stuart Hall (1997) usefully summarizes:

> We tend to think of power as always radiating in a single direction— from top to bottom—and coming from a specific source—the sovereign, the state, the ruling class and so on. For Foucault,

however, power does not "function in the form of a chain"—it circulates. It is never monopolized by one centre. It 'is deployed and exercised through a net-like organization'. This suggests that we are all, to some degree, caught up in its circulation—oppressors and oppressed. It does not radiate downwards, either from one source or from one place. Power relations permeate all levels of social existence and are therefore to be found operating at every site of social life—in the private spheres of the family and sexuality as much as in the public spheres of politics, the economy and the law. What's more, power is not only negative, repressing what it seeks to control. It is also productive. It 'doesn't only weigh on us as a force that says no, but … it traverses and produces things, it induces pleasure, forms of knowledge, produces discourse. It needs to be thought of as a productive network which runs through the whole social body'. (77)

Foucault argued that power is not simply negative. It is not like a hammer that comes down and says "no, you cannot do that." While it sometimes may operate in this way, Foucault pushes us to see the positive or productive aspects of power. By positive, he does not mean "good." Instead a focus on the positive or productive aspects of power seeks to show how power is also operating in our conceptions of liberation, empowerment, and freedom. How are our hopes, dreams, desires, pleasure and our very conceptions of Self bound up with the power relations characteristic of the society within which we live?

In her essay "Theory and Justice," Avery Gordon (2004) reminds us that the workings of power are much more nuanced and intricate than "the names we give to them suggest" (100). Describing a conception of power deeply informed by the work of Michel Foucault and his "microphysics of power," Gordon writes:

> Power can be invisible, it can be fantastic, it can be dull and routine, it can be grand and obvious. It can reach you by the baton of the police, it can speak in the language of your own thoughts and desires. It can feel like remote control, it can exhilarate like liberation. (100)

This insistence on the multiple registers through which power inflects the social world and our lives is vital for those engaged in creative writing.

The attempt to fix meaning is a central move of power. In her TED talk, "The Danger of a Single Story," Adichie argues that "power is the ability not just to tell the story of another person, but to make it the definitive story of that person." This speaks to the importance of an analysis of power in our writing and participation in the writing workshop.

Power relations traverse the creative writing workshop. At its root, politics is about power. An understanding of this renders the workshop space and creative writing fundamentally political. In a 1975 speech at Portland State University, Toni Morrison said the following,

> I do not make a distinction between politics and art in this sense. To me all of the best art is political, all of it, whether *Guernica* or *Anna Karenina*, it's all political ... it has to do with the society and what's wrong with it, and methods for its correction. Also I do not make a distinction between the artist and the other world,

the "real" so-called work-a-day world. I do not subscribe to the theory of the artist as a sort of separate aesthetic being in the ivory tower suffering and talking about beauty. It is work, hard work and there's a lot of it, and there's a lot of it that needs to be done, but that's exactly what it is. It is not sitting under willow trees and being inspired et cetera ... It has something to do with work. I am not sure that it's better work, as a matter of fact, than any other kind of work. I'm not convinced that it is. I think it has been handled and received more elegantly, but I'm not sure that it's better. I'm not sure that I wouldn't be just as happy if I were capable, and I am not, of making one perfect chair that would hold a human body properly. And I approach my work the same way I expect chair-makers to approach theirs.

If I'm gon' make a chair I have to find out about the wood, huh? Know all about my craft. I have to look at the human body, see how it looks when folded into a seated position, try to construct a chair that holds it et cetera, try to make it beautiful and comfortable, and try to make it long-lasting. And that's what writers ought to do: find out all they have to know about their craft. Instead of looking at lumber, they look at publishers. Find out all you need to know about that, and then do your work. And, nevertheless, as a human being you have responsibilities to the community, period. I don't care what you do, whether you make a chair or make a book. It doesn't separate you.

Differences can deepen participants' understanding of one another and the world, providing the springboard we need for critical, creative social change. The challenge today is to facilitate a workshop space where people of all racialized and ethnic groups, gender identities, religions, ages, sexual orientations, disabilities, socioeconomic backgrounds, regions, and nationalities are able to share their rich array of perspectives and experiences. This requires being aware of how one's words and actions can impact the community of learners. How do we hold the differing social locations and access to power of workshop participants? Some of us may have loved ones who have experienced violence at the hands of law enforcement. Some of us have sisters, brothers, mothers, and fathers who are currently locked up in state cages. Making our differences a creative resource entails an obligation to pay attention to how power works in the workshop. Who takes up space? Who has the authority to define good writing? It is vital to reflect on where one's privilege allows one to dominate, to take up more space, erase the experiences of other folks, and control what is thinkable. Conversely, we must be able to hold the simultaneity of oppression and privilege. In the workshop, participants must reflect on how marginalization might require that one work harder to make one's voice heard. The workshop can be a counter-space, a place where we can ask difficult questions with the understanding that we are all in the process of decolonizing our minds and bodies, and that we will make mistakes, which is fundamentally human. The important thing is to be gentle and loving with each other, even as you commit to caring about one another enough to challenge each other's complicity in systems of violence and oppression.

Privilege

Think about the rights and resources that you value, the rights and resources that are important to your flourishing. It is likely that the rights and resources that come to your mind are not shared by all: the right to safety or the right to clean water, for example.

Throughout history, groups of people have been excluded or barred from accessing rights and resources that others have had. Access to resources is not evenly distributed. We know, for instance, that people of color are more likely to be forced to "contend with dirty air and drinking water, and the location of noxious facilities such as municipal landfills, incinerators, hazardous waste treatment, storage and disposal facilities owned by private industry, government and even the military" (50), as Robert Bullard notes in "Confronting Environmental Racism in the 21st Century." Environmental racism, or the environmental harms that are disproportionately faced by people of color, is a form of institutional discrimination. Quoting Joe R. Feagin and Clarence B. Feagin, Bullard describes institutional racism as the "actions or practices carried out by members of dominant (racial or ethnic) groups that have differential and negative impacts on members of subordinate (racial and ethnic) groups" (qtd.

in Bullard 50). Certain rights and resources are available primarily to some, and not to others—and these rights and resources are forms of privilege.

The uneven distribution of privileges has been part of global history shaped by colonialism. Colonial powers have pillaged the land and the cultural legacies of people groups around the world. The colonial history of genocide, extraction, and subjugation continues today, and these histories have created intergenerational benefits for dominant groups. Thinking of the US context, Bullard notes how the nation "was founded on the principles of 'free land' (stolen from Native Americans and Mexicans), 'free labor' (African slaves brought to this land in chains) and 'free men' (only white men)" (50).

Kimberlé Crenshaw and Luke Harris, with the African American Policy Forum, have created an online video that illustrates this history. Called "The Unequal Opportunity Race," the video opens with four runners, lining up for the race of their lives. But only two of the runners—specifically the two runners who are white—are able to run when the gun first goes off. Slavery, genocide, broken treaties, and other crimes prevent the runners of color from getting the start that the white runners have. The time clock runs through the years of American history. When the runners of color are finally able to take off, they still face the obstacles of institutional discrimination. We come to see in the video that the system has determined the winners from the start.

A collection of papers from panels convened in the 1980s by the National Economic Association determined that in the United States, labor market discrimination, and the unpaid slave labor prior to 1863, the underpayment of African Americans since 1863, coupled with the denial of opportunity to buy land, is equivalent to the entire worth of the United States. In other words, the entire worth of the United States was stolen from African Americans who were forced to come to this country in the slave trade. And this statistic considers only one easily monetized way of looking at discrimination; it does not consider the forms of intergenerational trauma and the denial of access to resources such as quality schooling, and clean air and water. This statistic doesn't provide a broad picture of the many, interlocking forms of oppression that people around the globe face each day; it provides just one small window into the reality of our global history, and the ways that benefits have been granted to some at the literal and violent expense of others.

It's important to notice your own reactions when you are presented with information like this. Robin DiAngelo warns white readers who come to her books that "we have a deep interest in denying those forms of oppression that benefit us" (11). As Barbara Smith famously said, in her 1980 address to the National Women's Studies Association (which was subsequently published in the journal *Frontiers*), "The degree to which it is hard or uncomfortable for you to have the issue raised is the degree to which you know inside of yourself that you aren't dealing with the issue, the degree to which you are hiding from the oppression that undermines ... lives" (48).

DiAngelo describes privilege using the metaphor of a current of water. If we are benefactors of privilege, "the current in the water is going in our direction; the society is set up to affirm, accommodate, and reward the norms of our group. Anyone who has ever swum with a current knows that the current makes swimming so much easier" (69). It may still take effort to get where you are going, but you have help in getting there—help you may not always be able to measure or identify. If we are benefitting from the current, we may not notice it's there. It may be invisible and imperceptible to us. Indeed, as Peggy McIntosh notes in "White Privilege: Unpacking the Invisible Knapsack," those who benefit from privilege may be "meant to remain 'oblivious'" in a system that cloaks discrimination in a myth of meritocracy. In other words, the benefactors of systems of privilege have a vested interest in sustaining these forms of privilege and keeping them invisible. The myth that a person has access to rights and resources based solely on their individual merits helps to sustain those invisible systems of privilege. Gloria Yamato defines the myth of meritocracy in "Something about the Subject Makes It Hard to Name," an essay collected in *Making Face/Making Soul*: "The oppressors are purported to have an innate ability to access economic resources, information, respect, etc., while the oppressed are believed to have a correspondingly negative innate ability" (20).

DiAngelo notes that the metaphor of the river current is a limited way of describing privilege, in that it accounts for only one vector— the flow of one river. When we think about privilege, we need to account for the multiple intersecting forms of oppression that may be pushing against someone, or propelling another person along. Forms of oppression are interconnected. As Lee Anne Bell notes in an early chapter of *Readings for Diversity and Social Justice*, "No one form of oppression is the base for all others, yet all are connected within a system that makes them possible" (23). Bell continues, "Eradicating oppression ultimately requires struggle against all its forms" (23). Its forms include racism, classism, sexism, heterosexism, transgender oppression, religious oppression, ableism, anti-Semitism, xenophobia, ageism, and—animal studies theorists have argued— anthropocentrism. These terms denote "the disadvantage and injustice some people suffer ... because of the everyday practices of a well-intentioned liberal society," as Iris Marion Young notes. "Oppression in this sense is structural," Young explains, "rather than the result of a few people's choices or policies. Its causes are embedded in unquestioned norms, habits, and symbols, in the assumptions underlying institutional rules and the collective consequences of following those rules." Oppression is "a consequence of often unconscious assumptions and reactions of well-meaning people in ordinary interactions, media, and cultural stereotypes, and structural features of bureaucratic hierarchies and market mechanisms—in short, the normal processes of everyday life" (36).

The features of oppression have been cataloged by several theorists. Robin DiAngelo notes how oppression is complex (intricate and interconnected), pervasive (widespread through all societal domains), variable (changing and transforming to adapt to cultural shifts), persistent (prevailing over time and across places), severe (having serious consequences for individuals' lives), and power-based (benefiting some and restricting options for others).

Lee Anne Bell in "What Is Social Justice?" offers another list of defining features of oppression, noting that oppression is restrictive (denoting "structural and material constraints that significantly shape a person's life chances and sense of possibility"), hierarchical (meaning that "dominant or privileged groups reap advantage, often in unconscious ways, from the disempowerment of targeted groups"), and internalized (in that oppression resides not only in "external social institutions and norms but lodges in the human psyche as well" through conscious or unconscious attitudes or beliefs held by both those who benefit from oppressive regimes and those who are harmed by them).

Iris Marion Young observes "Five Faces of Oppression," or five conditions that are named under the heading of oppression; these are exploitation, marginalization, powerlessness, cultural imperialism, and violence.

These ways of understanding oppression, provided by DiAngelo, Bell, and Young, are meant to help us to name and uproot the forms of oppression that condition our world. Part of this work requires that we come to identify the forms of privilege that are not available to all, and that we allow this recognition to come to transform our institutionalized and day-to-day practices.

In creative writing, for example, we can unpack a number of privileges that are granted to some to the exclusion of others. Who gets published, who gets anthologized, who is counted as a legitimate writer, who gets represented in the stories we tell—all of these factors create systems of inequity within creative writing. To what extent are you aware of forms of discrimination in the publishing industry and in the creative writing workshop? To what extent are you aware of conversations taking place in online forums and elsewhere about the experiences of people of color in the workshop, including responses to Junot Díaz's "MFA vs. POC"? To what extent are you aware of disparities in who gets published and who gets hired onto editorial staffs, such as statistics offered by the VIDA Count? Do you recognize when white supremacy is reinforced, when whiteness gets symbolically attached to positive associations that confer dominance?

Do you notice when craft texts or creative writing instruction serves to sustain what Audre Lorde calls the "mythical norm," "usually defined as white, thin, male, young, heterosexual, christian, and financially secure" (116)? Lorde writes, "It is with this mythical norm that the trappings of power reside within society" (116).

We need to continue to develop tools for addressing the forms of oppression that operate in creative writing and in our world. These tools move beyond guilt or defensiveness or "white fragility." We remember James Baldwin's words: "I'm not interested in anybody's guilt. Guilt is a luxury that we can no longer afford. I know you didn't do it, and I didn't do it either, but I am responsible for it because I am a man and a citizen of this country and you are responsible for it, for the very same reason." We take this responsibility into our writing and into all that we do.

Race

While there are biological reasons behind people's physical appearance, human beings are not constituted by "races." Human beings are one race. However, questioning that fact has shaped the course of Western history for the past millennium. Debates about whether human beings are one race and the relationship between groups have been staged on the terrain of religion, science, and social theory. At the beginning of the twenty-first century, it is now commonly understood that race is a social construct. However, biological notions of race ("biologism") continue to circulate, often as the unspoken assumptions behind various political arguments. The study of "race"—and how groups have been and are racialized—is complex.

It is important to clarify the relationship between the terms "race" and "racism." A modern concept of race as a set of defined and innate features of a group is the product of racism. As Ta-Nehisi Coates writes in *Between the World and Me*, "Race is the child of racism, not the father" (7). Racism is the translation of that seemingly natural set of features (race) into a hierarchical system through which people's life chances are distributed. Stuart Hall notes that classification itself is not inherently problematic. Classification stabilizes a culture and is a central component of language. However, it is the coming together of classification and power that renders racism so very problematic. Racism "creates or reproduces structures of domination based on racial significations and identities" (Omi and Winant 2015, 128).

Essentialism is the view that things or people have a fixed set of characteristics that make them what they are—that they have an underlying/unchanging essence. An essentialist position regarding "race" conceives of it as something fixed, concrete, and objective. So, for example, statements such as "Black people are good at basketball" or "Asians can't drive" essentialize, or imply that a group has a fixed set of characteristics which are inherent and unchanging. Omi and Winant's definition above points to two central facets of racism: (1) essentialism and (2) that those essentialist ideas create or reproduce a system of power and subjection or "structure of domination." As we can see from Omi and Winant's definition, racism is hardly something that one individual can create and sustain alone. Thus, racism is systemic and transcends an individual's prejudice.

The use of the term "race" to describe distinct categories of people is surprisingly recent. In 1508, William Dunbar, a Scottish member of King James IV's court, wrote a poem called "The Dance of Sevin Deidly Sins." This poem is one of the earliest uses of the term "race" in the English language. One of the verses listed among those guilty of Envy was "bakbyttaruis of sindry racis"—backbiters of sundry races. Scholars have speculated that he borrowed "racis" from the Spanish word *raza*, which the Spanish applied to breeds of horses and dogs. Originally, "race" was used to think about tribe or lineage, and Dunbar employed race to mean family lineage in this early context. Darian-

Smith (2010) explains that between the sixteenth and eighteenth centuries religion would be a primary way of sorting difference and debating the concept of race. Las Casas and Sepulveda famously debated the question of race and the treatment of the colonized in the Valladolid debate in 1550. Held at the Colegio de San Gregorio, these debates demonstrate how the question of whether Indigenous peoples could be converted to Catholicism was central to the development of a modern notion of race.

It would not be until the advent of the Enlightenment that Europeans would begin to investigate the question of "race" from a scientific point of view. During the long nineteenth century, science increasingly became the terrain on which questions of difference were debated. Around the 1850s, the American theory of polygenism, the idea that there were "multiple, separate creations for each race as a distinct species ... enjoyed wide credence in international scientific circles" (Wallis 102). Louis Aggasiz had daguerreotypes taken of enslaved Africans to prove their racial inferiority. Samuel Morton collected hundreds of skulls from the graves of Indigenous peoples, publishing two skull "compendia": *Crania Americana* (1839) and *Crania Aegyptiaca* (1844). This period of scientific racism, where the bodies of women, people of color, and other marginalized groups were measured, dissected, and cataloged, still has a profound impact on the meaning of science, power, and knowledge. Moreover, people of color are still impacted by the racialized images internalized from the larger culture and can hold racist views toward other racialized groups and their own communities.

Many scholars use the terminology of "racialized groups" rather than "races" in order to avoid reifying or stabilizing the idea of race in the very language we use to talk about the problem. The use of "racialized" points to this as a process (-ization) by which people are sorted into racial hierarchies. But how does this process work? The late Black British scholar, Stuart Hall, charted the discursive character of "race," calling it a "floating signifier." Floating because racial meanings change across time and place. Racial meanings are "constantly being transformed by political struggle" (Omi and Winant 2015, 110). Hall used the term "signifier" to name the discursive character of "race." If "we are readers of race ... it works like a language."

So, if race works like a language, we are led to ask: how does language work? The linguist Ferdinand de Saussure shows that signification or the sign is the central fact of language. The sign is made up of a signifier and signified (signifier = the form; signified = the idea or concept with which the form is associated). In explaining Saussure's ideas here, Jonathan Culler (1976) writes:

> Language is a system of signs. Noises count as language only when they serve to express or communicate ideas; otherwise they are just noise. And to communicate ideas they must be part of a system of conventions, part of a system of signs. The sign is the union of a form which signifies, which Saussure calls the *signifiant* or signifier, and an idea signified, the *signifé* or signified. Though we may speak of signifier and signified as if they were separate entities, they exist only as components of the sign. The sign is the central fact of language. (19)

So, for example, the signifier or form "=" is associated with the signified "equals." The two parallel lines stand in for the idea of equal. In his famous lecture "Race: A Floating Signifier," Stuart Hall argues that this is how race works, "race is more like a language than it is like the way in which we are biologically constituted." Bodily racial signifiers include things like skin color, hair, the shape of one's nose. Additionally, things like the way someone talks, articles of clothing, and types of cars get racialized and associated with particular racialized groups. Hall poignantly argues that we are readers of race, that the body is text that we read, inferring all types of ideas based on a variety of signifiers.

From Hall's work, we can see that systems of racial thought are, in a certain sense, fictions. However, they are assemblages through which power takes up the body. Race is a construct that has material consequences on people's lives. Referring to race as a device, the character Tshembe in Lorraine Hansberry's *Les Blancs* puts it this way: "I believe in the recognition of devices as *devices*—but I also believe in the reality of those devices." The device called race is a fiction, "but the fact remains that a man ... who is lynched in Mississippi because he is black—is suffering the utter reality of that device of conquest." So, to paraphrase Tshembe, even if race is a lie—i.e., a fabricated construct— race still exists in that it is taken up and used in real, material ways. Foregrounding the material consequences of racism, Ruth Wilson Gilmore (2007) defines racism as "group-differentiated vulnerability to premature death" (28).

These real, material effects of racism tell us that there is no such thing as "color-blindness." Race is a fiction, but it is not an illusion. One might have been taught to deny race in grade school; a person may have been taught to say that "I don't see race." However, this language of color-blindness supports white supremacy because it "removes from personal thought and public discussion any taint or suggestion of white supremacy ... while legitimating the existing social, political and economic arrangements which privilege whites" (Gallagher 26).

Likewise, the popular use of the concept of "reverse racism" demonstrates a fundamental misunderstanding of what racism is and the depth of subjection being named with that term. The popular notion of "reverse racism" fails to attend to power relations between groups. While racialized groups can hold a prejudice against white people, they can hardly be said to have constructed a system which uses those prejudices as a basis for resource distribution. Many critical race scholars use the terms "racism" and "white supremacy" interchangeably, as the primary systems of racism in the West contemporarily operate to privilege people categorized as white.

Creative writers participate in these discourses in the way that we represent people and communities. Understanding this discursive approach to race can allow us to be more thoughtful in constructing our narratives of power and people. There is no story or poem that is apart from race, and we must work to gain a deeper understanding of how race works in and upon our work. Books like Beth Loffreda and Claudia Rankine's *The Racial Imaginary* and Toni Morrison's *Playing in the Dark* go far in helping us to think about the role race plays in our writing, and we do well to keep race as a central topic of discussion in the workshop.

Religion

Literary production works in direct relation to religion. Indeed, the study of literature in the present-day English department has a history in the exegesis of sacred texts. Today's writers represent religious beliefs of their characters, as they may also draw upon foundational narratives in religion—Edenic myths and portrayals of a postlapsarian world, for example, or the Buddhist narrative structure of ground (ignorance), path (training), goal (realization of impermanence). Today's writers may draw upon older sacred texts that remain living and present to those who study them, embedding allusions to holy texts in new literary forms.

Literatures share in the key questions and themes of religion: death, conversion and ecstasy, love and evil, visions of the end, intermediality. Indeed, these are the themes that organize the book *Religion and Literature: A Reader*, edited by Robert Detwiler and David Jasper. Art and religion both offer interpretations of the spiritual and that which gives life meaning. Art and religion both heighten spiritual awareness, awakening us to the complexities and mysteries of the world, refusing to reduce reality to what can be empirically measured, predicted, and observed.

Writers may come to religious study in order to understand the key mysteries and complexities of our time. Each religious tradition has a set of canonical texts that exist as outgrowths of religious practice. In Hinduism, for example, there is the *Mahabharata* (and its embedded lyrical drama, the *Bhagavad Gita*), the *Ramayana*, and the play *Shakuntala*. A full understanding of these texts requires an understanding of their religious context, but it is important to also not limit the text to become only a flattened historical artifact of a cultural tradition. These texts are literary texts that open themselves to close reading and interpretation. We should be careful about reading the religious texts as a mere window into a static culture; instead we come to these texts with the understanding that practitioners are in active relationship with them, and they thus exceed any academic analysis.

Religion is tied to the beliefs, epistemologies, practices, rituals, and the emotional lives of groups of people, and therefore religious contexts overlap with cultural contexts. To respectfully read texts that represent diverse religions is to expand one's cultural literacy and one's cultural humility, understanding that one's own cultural vantage point is just one in an infinite array.

Religion provides one lens or frame for reading literature, and it also plays a key role in our understanding of identity. Religion can be a locus of discrimination and oppression. On the one hand, people may be discriminated against because of religious affiliation; on the other hand, prejudicial laws and practices (including the enslavement of African peoples, the eradication of Indigenous peoples) have been backed and undergirded by religious beliefs. Acts of genocide have been completed in the name of religion.

Stereotypical thinking about religion creates forms of prejudice, including Islamophobia and religious xenophobia. Religious practices are often misunderstood. Consider, for example, how words such as "guru," "nirvana," and "pundit" are used in Western culture. The Hindi meaning of "guru" is religious teacher, but the Western appropriation of this term exaggerates the term into a fanatical self-designated leader. "Nirvana" in the Hindi meaning points to freedom from the endless cycle of rebirth; it is a metaphysical term. However, the Western appropriation of the term turns it into a psychedelic ecstasy or drug-induced high, evacuating the term of its metaphysical significance. A "pundit" in Hindi is a religious scholar—someone who carefully studies, but some Western adoptions of this term radicalize it and use it to describe a "talking head" who is single-minded in preaching a particular political agenda. These discrepancies are charted by Rita Chaudhry Sethi in the essay "Smells Like Racism," which describes how "Eastern religions are commonly perceived as fraudulent, cultish, and fanatical; they are rarely perceived as equally legitimate as the spiritual doctrines of the Judeo-Christian tradition" (145).

As writers, we should work to interrogate the religious biases that may operate in our texts. How are we portraying religion and religious figures in our work, and are we offering representations in a way that is fully researched and mindful of religious oppression?

You may think of yourself as a solely "secular" writer, but, as Zhange Ni's essay "Postsecular Reading" shows, the religious and the secular are not "neatly bounded and easily separable entities" (51). By "postsecular reading," Zhange Ni refers to the need to perpetually "question the secular's claim to moral-political supremacy" and the need to challenge the "hegemonic universalism of 'secular' reason" (51). "Secular reasoning" is not superior to spiritually infused ways of knowing, and "secular reasoning" provides no universal framework shared by all.

Because it works against the antagonism toward religion that is present in some secular humanistic thought, Ni's "postsecular reading" operates in contrast to the theories of religion offered by thinkers such as Karl Marx who, in the "Contribution to the Critique of Hegel's Philosophy of Law" (1844), held that

> Religion is the self-consciousness and self-esteem of man who has either not yet found himself or has already lost himself again. […] Religion is the sigh of the oppressed creature, the heart of a heartless world, just as it is the spirit of spiritless conditions. It is the *opium* of the people. To abolish religion as the *illusory* happiness of the people is to demand their *real* happiness.

Postsecular reading, Zhange Ni says, "asks the reader to encounter the world and human lives as radically more than what secular modernity has made them … and to embrace a rigorous openness to the wholeness of reality, including the multiplicity of faith commitments, the alterity of religious traditions beyond the model of confessional communities, and the intertwined power relations of religion and politics" (52).

Some writers speak of their creative practice in spiritual terms, as they may consider the writing life to be a sacred calling or believe in supernatural "muses" who come to the aid of the literary writer. There is a long history in aesthetic theory that holds creation to be more about spiritual receptiveness than it is about intentional will. In these formulations, one receives the gift of the word, which comes from beyond oneself—one is merely a medium for creation. As you continue your study of creative writing, look for these spiritual ideas. This prioritization of mystery Mark McGurl finds to be "endemic to the discipline of creative writing whose ultimate commitment is not to knowledge but to what Donald Barthelme called 'Not-Knowing'" (qtd. in McGurl 9). McGurl continues, "The aura of literature must be protected at all costs, and the mysteries of the creative process must be explored without being dispelled" (10).

Contemporary creative writing is not unique in its regard for the importance of preserving a space for mystery. Aesthetic theories across different times and places have upheld a connection between aesthetic experience and the experience of the divine, while also refusing to instrumentalize art as theology's servant. Rasa theory, which derives from ancient Vedic literature, identifies "essences" of artforms that flower in the experience of art: Sringara (erotic sentiment, love), Hāsya (comic sentiment, mirth, playfulness), Karunarasa (pathetic sentiment, sorrow), Raudrarasa (furious sentiment), Virarasa (heroic sentiment, energy/action), Bhayanaka (the terrible, fear/terror), Bibhatsarasa (the odious, nausea, disgust), Adbhutarasa (the marvelous, awe, wonder), and Shanta (meditative peace). The capacities of the work of art, combined with the experience of the listener and the absence of distortion, can create a heightened emotional state and the experience of rasa. The singular rasa experience is pure, with no dust on the mirror of consciousness.

Creative writers can remain attentive to how theories of art-making from around the globe work in relation to religious and spiritual expression.

Representation

The Oxford English Dictionary suggests two relevant definitions of representation: 1. To represent something is to describe or depict it, to call it up in the mind by description or portrayal or imagination. 2. To represent also means to symbolize, stand for, to be a specimen of, or to substitute for.

Representation is the production of meaning through language. It is the act of representation, or representation as a practice, which produces culture. As Stuart Hall notes, "In language, we use signs and symbols—whether they are sounds, written words, electronically produced images, musical notes, even objects—to stand for or represent to other people our concepts, ideas and feelings. Language is one of the 'media' through which thoughts, ideas and feelings are represented in a culture." Representation is how we communicate meaning and build culture.

In his canonical tome, *Representation: Cultural Representations and Signifying Practices*, Stuart Hall highlights three approaches to representation. First, there is the reflective approach to representation, which sees language as simply reflecting meanings that already exist out in the world independent of the act of representation.

Representations mirror reality back to us as a form of *mimesis* or imitation. Such a perspective tends to rely on criteria of objectivity and universality (i.e., "Is this an accurate representation of X?"). Second, Hall notes the intentional approach to representation. The hallmark of this approach is a focus on the intentions of the author, as the name suggests. This theory of representation views language as expressing only what the author wants to say, their personally intended meaning. Finally, one can take a constructivist approach to representation, viewing meaning as constructed *in and through* language. It is this final and third theory of representation which has become dominant with the cultural turn in the humanities and social sciences. Such an approach refuses a view of representation which essentializes meaning, or reduces meaning to the author's intentions. Constructivist approaches destabilize the notion of representation as a transparent record of "reality," and instead show how conceptions of reality are established, reworked, and circulated. We construct the world and its meaning through the systems of representation we deploy. The naturalization of some representations of the world is a function of power and we should take it as our task to unpack how some representations come to be common sense, while others are ruled out or made unthinkable within particular contexts.

Representation is ultimately a question of power. Who represents? And who is represented? Taking an intersectional approach to creative writing asks us to question how dominance is conferred and perpetuated through representation. Too often marginalized groups become canvases upon which those with more power represent themselves. As Margaret Andersen and Patricia Hill Collins note regarding the omission of marginalized groups from the canon,

By minimizing the experiences and creations of these different groups, we communicate that their work and creativity is less important and less central to the development of culture than is the history of White American men ... Dominant narratives can try to justify the oppression of different groups, but the unwritten, untold subordinated truth can be a source of knowledge in pursuit of social justice. (14–15)

When marginalized groups are represented, it has often been in stereotypical ways. Patricia Hill Collins (2000) uses the vocabulary of "controlling images" to unearth the images of Black women in white supremacist culture. She highlights four images, which have been central to the gendered racism facing Black women: the Mammy, the Matriarch, the Welfare Queen, and the Jezebel. Collins writes, "Taken together, these prevailing images of Black womanhood represent elite White male interests in defining Black women's sexuality and fertility. Moreover, by meshing smoothly with intersecting oppressions of race, class, gender, and sexuality, they help justify the social practices that characterize the matrix of domination in the United States" (84).

Stuart Hall (1997) unpacks stereotyping as a representational practice, noting that it "reduces people to a few, simple, essential characteristics, which are represented as fixed by Nature" (257).

It is important to differentiate between typing and stereotyping (Dyer 1977). Categorization itself is not inherently problematic. We fit things into types to make sense of the world. This is central to meaning-making. Hall distinguishes this kind of general categorization from the representational practice of stereotyping:

Stereotypes get hold of a few "simple, vivid, memorable, easily grasped and widely recognized" characteristics about a person, *reduce* everything about the person to those traits, *exaggerate* and simplify them, and *fix* them without change or development to eternity .... *Stereotyping reduces, essentializes, naturalizes and fixes "difference."* (258)

Control over the representation of marginalized groups is central to the maintenance of any system of domination. The objective of stereotypes is "not to reflect or represent a reality but to function as a disguise, or mystification, of objective social relations" (Carby 22).

Ultimately, representation governs what becomes imaginable, and this renders representation a central concern for social justice. Highlighting the centrality of representation for a politics of anti-racism, bell hooks (1992) writes,

If we compare the relative progress African Americans have made in education and employment to the struggle to gain control over how we are represented, particularly in the mass media, we see that there has been little change in the area of representation. Opening a magazine or book, turning on the television set, watching a film, or looking at photographs in public spaces, we are most likely to see images of black people that reinforce and reinscribe white supremacy. Those images may be constructed by white people who have not divested of racism, or by people of color/ black people who may see the world through the lens of white supremacy-internalized racism. Clearly, those of us committed to black liberation struggle, to the freedom and self-determination of all black people, must face daily the tragic reality that we have collectively made few, if any, revolutionary interventions in the area of race and representation. (1–2)

Hooks's naming of internalized racism is significant here. Representation is not simply a question of how dominant groups view the marginalized, but also how those with less power come to view themselves. To be subject to dehumanizing images of one's own group is to be subject to, in Stuart Hall's words (2014), "the power to make us see and experience *ourselves* as 'Other.'"

Representation is a key site of struggle for social justice. As bell hooks (1992) writes,

From what political perspective do we dream, look, create, and take action? For those of us who dare to desire differently, who seek to look away from the conventional ways of seeing blackness and ourselves, the issue of race and representation is not just a question of critiquing the *status quo*. It is also about transforming the image, creating alternatives, asking ourselves questions about what types of images subvert, pose critical alternatives, and transform our worldviews and move us away from dualistic thinking about good and bad. Making a space for the transgressive image, the outlaw rebel vision, is essential to any effort to create a context for transformation. (4)

This helps us to understand the renaissance of Black mediamakers at the beginning of the twenty-first century. People of color working in film and television, such as Ava DuVernay and Shonda Rhimes, are challenging white supremacy in representations of people of color in ways that reshape and refigure the very terrain of the thinkable. It matters who the moviemakers are; it matters who holds the gatekeeping positions in an industry. Writers are calling for diversity in representation both in terms of who gets published and who does the publishing. Essays such as Rachel Deahl's "Why Publishing Is So White" and Chris Jackson's "Widening the Gates: Why Publishing Needs Diversity" reflect on the white-centric publishing industry: it is primarily white people who are hired and retained as editors in the industry. Antonio Aiello's "Equity in Publishing: What Should Editors Be Doing?"; Camille Rankine's "What's in a Number"; Matthew Salesses's "We Need Diverse Diverse Books"; and Daniel José Older's "Diversity Is Not Enough" are essays that reflect on how the biases of a white-dominated publishing industry create roadblocks in the pathway to publication for writers of color. Daniel José Older writes of the

> many interactions I'd had with agents—all but two of them white—before I landed with mine. The ones that said they loved my writing but didn't connect with the character, the ones that didn't think my book would be marketable even though it was already accepted at a major publishing house. I thought about the ones that wanted me to delete moments when a character of color gets mean looks from white people because "that doesn't happen anymore" and the white magazine editor who lectured me on how I'd gotten my own culture wrong. My friends all have the same stories of whitewashed covers and constant sparring with the many micro- and mega-aggressions of the publishing industry.

Older lists here just a fraction of the forms of bias and prejudice that show up in the publishing industry. Representation matters. The call is an urgent one. Writers can engage the "outlaw rebel vision" articulated by bell hooks and produce work that troubles dominant representations.

Sexuality

The history of the keyword "sexuality" reveals that it has found meaning in and through a range of other categories, including race and nation. While sexuality is often thought of in biological and fixed terms, critical intellectuals have placed this naturalization in question. Critical theory has shown how notions of sexuality are founded on socially constructed divisions between the normal and abnormal. Thus, sexuality has been revealed as a key site of political struggle and a terrain defined by oppression, power, and resistance. As Lisa Duggan writes in *Sex Wars: Sexual Dissent and Political Culture,* "conflicts over the politics of sexuality continue to occupy center stage in the United States. In addition, U.S.-based institutions and agencies have increasingly exported U.S.-style sexual politics across the globe" (Duggan and Hunter xiii). A critical interrogation of the politics of sexuality is vital for creative writers.

The philosopher Michel Foucault argued that a new understanding of sexuality arose in the late nineteenth century. As Siobhan Somerville (1999) writes,

Although sexual acts between two people of the same sex had been punishable during earlier periods through legal and religious sanctions, these sexual practices did not necessarily define individuals as homosexual per se. Only in the late nineteenth century did a new understanding of sexuality emerge in which sexual acts and desires became constitutive of identity. Homosexuality as the condition, and therefore the identity, of particular bodies was thus a historically specific production. (2–3)

This new understanding located sexuality within the individual, defining the sexual acts an individual engaged in as a fundamental part of their personhood and identity. Foucault argues that along with this new understanding of sexuality was "the repressive hypothesis," the supposition that sexuality was repressed and in need of liberation. This idea remains in circulation into the present. Foucault shows that during the late nineteenth century, rather than being repressed, sexuality underwent "an incitement to discourse." Sexuality became incessantly talked about, studied, catalogued, and managed.

The emergence of a modern notion of sexuality as a core part of identity is at the heart of power relations. Dean Spade and Craig Willse (2016) explain the centrality of normalization in Foucault's notion of disciplinary power:

Disciplinary power, power that establishes norms of good behavior and ideas about proper and improper categories of subjects. Disciplinary practices congeal in certain institutional locations such as the school, the factory and the clinic, where proper behavior is codified at the level of detail, and subjects are formed to police ourselves and each other according to these norms (Foucault 1990). Feminist activists and scholars have accounted for the development of this kind of normalizing power, and how this power works both through institutions (including families, schools, and hospitals) and through the internalization of these norms within the subjects of those institutions. The invention of various categories of proper and improper subjects, such as categories of sexual deviants, is a key feature of disciplinary power. Creating these types or categories of people requires establishing and maintaining guidelines and norms that guide the process of diagnosing or labeling. (553–554)

The concept of normalization is useful for understanding the way that power relations take hold of and proliferate ideas about sexuality here. Normalization is the mechanism by which heterosexism and homophobia are generated. Heterosexism, the institutionalized power and privilege accorded to heterosexual behavior and identification, defines heterosexuality as the norm (Andersen and Collins 84). This normalization of heterosexuality produces a category of homosexual, which becomes marked as abnormal, pathological, and excluded. This constitutes homophobia, the fear and hatred of homosexuality.

An intersectional approach is vital to understanding sexuality. Without a robust understanding of the politics of sexuality, we cannot see precisely how colonialism and enslavement were achieved. As Margaret L. Andersen and Patricia Hill Collins (2016) write, "Historically racism has been buttressed by beliefs about Black sexuality" (71). Joey Mogul, Andrea Ritchie, and Kay Whitlock also unpack this idea that racism and systems of sexual normalization buttress each other. In *Queer (In)justice: The Criminalization of LGBT People in the United States*, Mogul, Ritchie, and Whitlock show how Indigenous people, people of African descent, and immigrants have all been linked historically to constructions of deviant sexuality.

Racism and heterosexism have both relied on segregation, enforced by the state as a central locus of power. By adopting an intersectional perspective, we can see that systems of oppression rely on one another, share histories and technologies of domination.

An intersectional understanding of sexuality has been pushed forward over the past few decades by the overlapping fields of women of color feminisms and queer studies. The term "queer" is in usage in popular and academic discourses with a variety of valences. Queer is both used as an umbrella term for LGBT identities, as well as a critique of the seeming stability of identity categories based on sexual orientation. "To queer" something becomes a critique where queering means the destabilization of assumed categories. In this way, the verb "queer" has become an analytic method within the academy. In popular usages, the term "queer" often contains hints of this notion of troubling or destabilizing normative orders. Thus, queer signals a denaturalization of categories, such as "gay," "lesbian," and "straight"— an insistence on the cultural, social, and historical construction of these categories rather than an understanding of them as immutable, essential identities. Scholars of queer theory often refuse to provide a linear account of its origins, thus queering the search for a definitive accounting of the term itself.

From about the seventeenth century until well into the twentieth century, the term "queer" was used as a synonym for strange, odd, or peculiar, with a particular negative implication. Uses in early twentieth century African American literature of the term "queer" show us the imbrication of race and sexuality. In both Nella Larson's *Passing* and Jean Toomer's *Cane*, the term is used to name sexual deviance alongside racial ambiguity. As Siobhan Somerville writes, "The term could also carry racialized meanings, particularly in the context of mixed-race identities that exposed the instability of divisions between 'black' and 'white'" (188).

The notion of a queer aesthetic articulated in Barrie Jean Borich's 2012 *Brevity Magazine* essay "The Craft of Writing Queer" is useful in beginning to imagine the possibilities of this keyword for creative writers:

> What if all nonfiction writers imagined a queer aesthetic at the center of our discourse? By queer aesthetic I mean not just the work of queer authors but all voices and forms that are equally open to pleasure and injury, that are not afraid of the body, that are both sex-positive and self-critical, that are as interested in intersections and critique as they are in the personal politics of memory. Work that does not hold to sentimental definitions of love, marriage, monogamy, childrearing, family, and friendship; work that is as explicit and confessional as it needs to be, withholding only for reasons of flow, impact, and design rather than to uphold community, intellectual, or art-world standards; work that breaks rather than maintains codes, doesn't keep secrets to retain power, is eager to pay debts and reveal the means and archives of its own production.

A critical orientation toward sexuality and a commitment to queering race, gender, sexuality, and other nodes of exclusion holds a central value in the liberatory creative writing workshop.

BIBLIOGRAPHY AND SUGGESTED READINGS

"Community, n." *OED Online*. Oxford University Press. Accessed June 14, 2018. Web. www.oed.com/view/Entry/37337. Accessed August 31, 2018.

"Diaspora, n." *OED Online*. Oxford University Press. Accessed June 14, 2018. Web. www.oed.com/view/Entry/52085. Accessed September 1, 2018.

Abdulhadi, Rabab. "Where Is Home? Fragmented Lives, Border Crossings, and the Politics of Exile." *Radical History Review* 86, no. 1 (2003): 89–101.

Acker, Joan. *Class Questions: Feminist Answers*. Oxford, UK: Rowman & Littlefield, 2006.

Adichie, Chimamanda Ngozi. "The Danger of a Single Story." 2009. TED Talk. Accessed June 14, 2018. Web. https://www.ted.com/talks/chimamanda_adichie_the_danger_of_a_single_story?language=en.

African American Policy Forum (AAPF). "Shortened Lifespan." September 22, 2018. Web. http://www.aapf.org/shortened-lifespan/

Ahmad, Aijaz. "Jameson's Rhetoric of Otherness and the 'National Allegory.'" *Social Text* 17 (Autumn 1987): 3–25.

Ahmed, Sara. *The Cultural Politics of Emotion*. Edinburgh: Edinburgh University Press, 2004.

Ahmed, Sara. *On Being Included: Racism and Diversity in Institutional Life*. Durham, NC: Duke University Press, 2012.

Ahmed, Sara. *The Promise of Happiness*. Durham, NC: Duke University Press, 2010.

Ahmed, Sara. *Queer Phenomenology: Orientations, Objects, Others*. Durham, NC: Duke University Press, 2006.

Aiello, Atonio. "Equity in Publishing: What Should Editors Be Doing?" *PEN American*. October 24, 2015. Accessed November 20, 2018. Web. https://pen.org/equity-in-publishing-what-should-editors-be-doing/

Aitken, Neil. *De-Canon Reading List*. Accessed February 2, 2018. Web. www.de-canon.com

Alexander, M. Jacqui. *Pedagogies of Crossing: Meditations on Feminism, Sexual Politics, Memory, and the Sacred*. Durham, NC: Duke University Press, 2006.

Althusser, Louis. "Ideology and Ideological State Apparatuses (Notes Towards an Investigation)." In *The Anthropology of the State: A Reader*, edited by Aradhana Sharma and Akhil Gupta, 86–111. Oxford: Blackwell, 2006.

Anderson, Benedict. *Imagined Communities: Reflections on the Origin and Spread of Nationalism*. London, UK: Verso Books, 2006.

Andersen, Margaret L., and Patricia Hill Collins. *Race, Class and Gender: An Anthology*, 9th edition. Boston, MA: Cengage Learning, 2016.

Anthias, Floya. "New Hybridities, Old Concepts: The Limits of 'Culture.'" *Ethnic and Racial Studies* 24, no. 4 (2001): 619–641.

Anzaldúa, Gloria. *Borderlands/La Frontera: The New Mestiza*, 1st edition. San Francisco, CA: Aunt Lute Books, 1987.

Anzaldúa, Gloria, ed. *Making Face, Making Soul/Haciendo Caras: Creative and Critical Perspectives by Feminists of Color*. San Francisco, CA: Aunt Lute Books, 1995.

Appiah, Kwame Anthony. Modern Language Association Presidential Address: Boundaries of Culture. 2017 MLA Convention. Philadelphia, PA. 2017. Accessed June 12, 2018. Web. www.mla.org/Convention/Convention-History/MLA-Presidential-Addresses/

Aristotle. *Metaphysics*. Indianapolis, IN: Hackett Publishing, 2016.

Ashcroft, Bill, Gareth Griffiths, and Helen Tiffin. *Post-Colonial Studies: The Key Concepts*. New York: Routledge, 2013.

"Authenticity, n." *OED Online*. Oxford University Press. Accessed June 14, 2018. Web. http://www.oed.com/view/Entry/13325?redirectedFrom=authenticity

Baird, J. L. "En-abled Poetry." *Kaleidoscope* 7 (1983): 3–5.

Baird, J. L., and Deborah S. Workman. *Toward Solomon's Mountain: The Experience of Disability in Poetry*. Philadelphia, PA: Temple University Press, 1986.

Baldwin, James. "Words of a Native Son." In *The Price of the Ticket: Collected Nonfiction, 1948–1985*. New York: St. Martin's Press, 1985.

Barthes, Roland. *Image-Music-Text*. New York: Noonday, 1988.

Bartlett, Jennifer, Sheila Black, and Michael Northen, eds. *Beauty Is a Verb: The New Poetry of Disability*. El Paso, TX: Cinco Puntos, 2011.

Bauman, Zygmunt. *Globalization: The Human Consequences*. New York: Columbia University Press, 1998.

Bawarshi, Anis. "Between Genres: Uptake, Memory, and U.S. Public Discourse on Israel-Palestine." In *Genre and the Performance of Publics*, edited by Mary Jo Reiff and Anis Bawarshi, 43–59. Logan: Utah State University Press/University of Colorado Press, 2016.

Beardsley, Monroe C. *Aesthetics: From Classical Greece to the Present*. Tuscaloosa: University of Alabama Press, 1966.

Bell, Chris. "Introducing White Disability Studies: A Modest Proposal." In *The Disability Studies Reader*, 2nd edition, edited by Lennard J Davis, 275–283. New York: Routledge, 2006.

Bell, Lee Anne. "Theoretical Foundations." In *Readings for Diversity and Social Justice*, 3rd edition, edited by Maurianne Adams, Warren J. Blumenfeld, Heather W. Hackman, Madeline L. Peters, and Ximena Zuniga, 35–45. New York: Routledge, 2013.

Benjamin, Bret. *Invested Interests: Capital, Culture, and the World Bank*. Minneapolis: University of Minnesota Press, 2007.

Bennett, Tony, Lawrence Grossberg, and Meaghan Morris. *New Keywords: A Revised Vocabulary of Culture and Society*. Malden, MA: John Wiley & Sons, 2013.

Berlant, Lauren. *The Female Complaint: The Unfinished Business of Sentimentality in American Culture*. Durham, NC: Duke University Press, 2008.

Bhabha, Homi K. *The Location of Culture*. London: Routledge, 1994.

Bhabha, Homi K., ed. *Nation and Narration*. London: Routledge, 1990.

Bigelow, Susan Jane. "A Trans Author on Writing a Trans Character." BookRiot. June 28, 2016. Accessed April 1, 2019. Web. https://bookriot.com/2016/06/28/a-trans-author-on-writing-a-trans-character/

Blackmore, Susan J. *Consciousness. A Very Short Introduction*. Oxford: Oxford University Press, 2017.

Bordo, Susan. *Unbearable Weight: Feminism, Western Culture and the Body*. Berkeley, CA, Los Angeles, and London: University of California Press, 1995.

Borich, Barrie Jean. "The Craft of Writing Queer." *Brevity Magazine*. September 17, 2012. Accessed September 8, 2018. Web. https://brevitymag.com/craft-essays/the-craft-of-writing-queer/

Bosworth, M., and J. Flavin *Race, Gender, and Punishment: From Colonialism to the War on Terror*. New Brunswick, NJ: Rutgers University Press, 2007.

Bourdieu, Pierre. *Distinction: A Social Critique of the Judgement of Taste*. International reprinting edition, translated by Tony Bennett. New York: Routledge Classics, 2010.

Bozarth, Alla Renée. *Lifelines: Threads of Grace through Seasons of Change*. New York: Sheed & Ward, 1995.

Brah, Avtar. *Cartographies of Diaspora: Contesting Identities* (Gender, Racism, Ethnicity Series). London: Routledge, 1996.

Brand, Dionne. *A Map to the Door of No Return: Notes to Belonging*. Toronto: Doubleday Canada, 2001.

Brennan, Teresa. *The Transmission of Affect*. Ithaca, NY: Cornell University Press, 2004.

Brenneis, Donald. "Shared and Solitary Sentiments: The Discourse of Friendship, Play, and Anger in Bhatgaon." In *Language and the Politics of Emotion*, edited by Lila Abu-Lughod and Catherine A. Lutz, 113–125. Cambridge: Cambridge University Press, 1990.

Brier, Evan. *A Novel Marketplace: Mass Culture, the Book Trade, and Postwar American Fiction*. Philadelphia: University of Pennsylvania Press, 2009.

Brush, Lisa D. *Gender and Governance*. Lanham, MD: Altamira Press, 2003.

Buchanan, Ian. *A Dictionary of Critical Theory* (Oxford Quick Reference). Oxford, UK: Oxford University Press, 2010.

Bullard, Robert D. "Confronting Environmental Racism in the 21st Century." *Race, Poverty & the Environment* 10, no. 1 (Summer 2003): 49–52.

Burke, Kenneth. *Counter-Statement*. Berkeley: University of California Press, 1968.

Burroway, Janet, Elizabeth Stuckey-French, and Ned Stuckey-French. *Writing Fiction: A Guide to Narrative Craft*, 9th edition. New York: Pearson, 2014.

Butler, Judith. "Critically Queer." *GLQ* 1 (1993): 17–32.

Butler, Judith. *Frames of War*. New York: Verso, 2010.

Butler, Judith. "Performative Acts and Gender Constitution: An Essay in Phenomenology and Feminist Theory." *Theatre Journal* 40, no. 4 (1988): 519–531.

Butler, Judith, and Gayatri Chakravorty Spivak. *Who Sings the Nation-State?: Language, Politics, Belonging*. London: Seagull Books, 2010.

Butler, Judith, and Joan Wallach Scott. *Feminists Theorize the Political*. New York: Routledge, 1992.

Byrd, J. A. *The Transit of Empire: Indigenous Critiques of Colonialism*. Minneapolis: University of Minnesota Press, 2011.

Calhoun, Craig. "'Belonging' in the Cosmopolitan Imaginary." *Ethnicities* 3, no. 4 (2003): 531–553.

Carby, Hazel V. *Reconstructing Womanhood: The Emergence of the Afro-American Woman Novelist*. Oxford: Oxford University Press, 1987.

Cariou, Warren. "Edgework: Indigenous Poetics as Re-Placement." In *Indigenous Poetics in Canada*, edited by Neal McLeod, 31–38. Wilfrid Laurier University Press, 2014.

Cassia, Paul Sant. "When Intuitive Knowledge Fails: Emotion, Art and Resolution." *Mixed Emotions: Anthropological Studies of Feeling*, edited by Kay Milton and Maruška Svašek, 109–126. Oxford: Berg, 2005.

Castells, Manuel. *The Rise of the Network Society*. Malden, MA: Blackwell, 1996.

Césaire, Aimé. *Discourse on Colonialism*. New York: Monthly Review Press, 2001.

Chandra, Vikram. "The Cult of Authenticity." *Boston Review*. February 1, 2000. Accessed August 8, 2018. Web. http://bostonreview.net/vikram-chandra-the-cult-of-authenticity

Cherniavsky, Eva. "Body." In *Keywords for American Cultural Studies*, edited by Bruce Burgett and Glenn Hendler. New York: New York University Press, 2007.

Cho, Sumi, Kimberlé Williams Crenshaw, and Leslie McCall. "Toward a Field of Intersectionality Studies: Theory, Applications, and Praxis." *Signs: Journal of Women in Culture and Society* 38, no. 4 (2013): 785–810.

Clare, Eli. *Exile and Pride: Disability, Queerness, and Liberation*. Durham, NC: Duke University Press, 2015.

Clark, Vèvè A. "Developing Diaspora Literacy and Marasa Consciousness." *Theatre Survey* 50, no. 1 (2009): 9–18.

Coates, Ta-Nehisi. *Between the World and Me*. New York: Spiegel & Grau, 2015.

Cohen, Cathy J. *The Boundaries of Blackness: AIDS and the Breakdown of Black Politics*. Chicago: University of Chicago Press, 1999.

Cohen, Cathy. "Punks, Bulldaggers, and Welfare Queens: The Radical Potential of Queer Politics." *GLQ: A Journal of Lesbian and Gay Studies* 3, no. 4 (1997): 437–465.

Cohen, Robin. *Global Diasporas: An Introduction*. New York: Routledge, 2008.

Cohen, Robin. "Solid, Ductile and Liquid: Changing Notions of Homeland and Home in Diaspora Studies." *Transnationalism: Diasporas and the Advent of a New (Dis)order*, edited by Eliezer Ben-Rafael and Yitzhak Sternberg, 117–134. New York: Brill, 2009.

Collins, Jim. *Bring on the Books for Everybody: How Literary Culture Become Popular Culture*. Durham, NC: Duke University Press, 2010.

Collins, Patricia Hill. *Black Feminist Thought: Knowledge, Consciousness, and the Politics of Empowerment*, 2nd edition. London: Routledge, 2000.

Collins, Patricia Hill. "It's All in the Family: Intersections of Gender, Race, and Nation." *Hypatia* 13, no. 3 (1998): 62–82.

Collins, Patricia Hill, and Sirma Bilge. *Intersectionality (Key Concepts)*. Cambridge: Polity, 2016.

Combahee River Collective. "The Combahee River Collective Statement." In *Words of Fire: An Anthology of African American Feminist Thought*, edited by Beverly Guy-Sheftall, 232–240. New York: The New Press, 1995.

Connell, Raewyn W. *Gender and Power*. Stanford, CA: Stanford University Press, 1987.

Coombe, Rosemary J. "The Properties of Culture and the Possession of Identity: Postcolonial Struggle and the Legal Imagination." In *Borrowed Power: Essays on Cultural Appropriation*, edited by Bruce Ziff and Pratima V. Rao, 74–97. New Brunswick, NJ: Rutgers, 1997.

Cooper, Brittney. "Intersectionality." In *The Oxford Handbook of Feminist Theory*, edited by Lisa Jane Disch and Mary E Hawkesworth. New York: Oxford University Press, 2016.

Coulthard, Glen Sean. *Red Skin, White Masks: Rejecting the Colonial Politics of Recognition*. Minneapolis: University of Minnesota Press, 2014.

Crenshaw, Kimberlé. "Demarginalizing the Intersection of Race and Sex: A Black Feminist Critique of Antidiscrimination Doctrine, Feminist Theory and Antiracist Politics." University of Chicago Legal Forum 1989, no. 1 (1989): 139–167.

Crenshaw, Kimberlé. "Mapping the Margins: Intersectionality, Identity Politics, and Violence against Women of Color." *Stanford Law Review* 43, no. 6 (1991): 1241–1299.

Crenshaw, Kimberlé, and Luke Harris, dir. *The Unequal Opportunity Race, 2010*. African American Policy Forum. Accessed June 12, 2018. Web. https://www. youtube.com/watch?v=vX_Vzl-r8NY

Cruikshank, Barbara. *The Will to Empower: Democratic Citizens and Other Subjects*. Ithaca, NY: Cornell University Press, 1999.

Csordas, Thomas J. *Body/Meaning/Healing*. New York: Palgrave Macmillan, 2002.

Culler, Jonathan D. *Ferdinand De Saussure*. Fontana, WI: Collins, 1976.

Culler, Jonathan D. *Literary Theory: A Very Short Introduction*. Oxford: Oxford University Press, 2011.

Dagnino, Arianna. *Transcultural Writers and Novels in the Age of Global Mobility*. West Lafayette, IN: Purdue University Press, 2015.

Damasio, Antonio. *The Feeling of What Happens: Body and Emotion in the Making of Consciousness*. San Diego: Harcourt, 1999.

Danius, Sara, and Stefan Jonsson. "An Interview with Gayatri Chakravorty Spivak." *Boundary 2* 20, no. 2 (Summer 1993): 24–50.

Darian-Smith, Eve. *Religion, Race, Rights: Landmarks in the History of Anglo-American Law*. Oxford: Hart Publishing, 2010.

Davidson, Michael. *Concerto for the Left Hand: Disability and the Defamiliar Body*. Ann Arbor: University of Michigan Press, 2008.

Deahl, Rachel. "Why Publishing Is So White." *Publisher's Weekly*. March 14, 2016. Accessed November 20, 2018. Web. https://www.publishersweekly. com/pw/by-topic/industry-news/publisher-news/article/69653-why-publishing-is-so-white.html

Deleuze, Gilles. "What Can a Body Do." In *Expressionism in Philosophy: Spinoza*. Brooklyn, NY: Zone Books, 1992.

Deleuze, Gilles, and Félix Guattari. *Kafka: Toward a Minor Literature*. Minneapolis: University of Minnesota Press, 1986.

Detwiler, Robert, and David Jasper, eds. *Religion and Literature: A Reader*. Louisville: Westminster John Knox Press, 2004.

Dewey, John. *Art as Experience*. New York: Perigee, 2005.

DiAngelo, Robin. *What Does It Mean to Be White?: Developing White Racial Literacy*. New York: Peter Lang, 2016.

Díaz, Junot. "MFA vs POC." *The New Yorker*. April 30, 2014. Accessed June 18, 2018. Web. https://www.newyorker.com/books/page-turner/mfa-vs-poc

Disch, Lisa Jane, and Mary E Hawkesworth. *The Oxford Handbook of Feminist Theory*. New York: Oxford University Press, 2016.

Dobyns, Stephen. *Best Words, Best Order*, 2nd edition. New York: Palgrave Macmillan, 2003.

Du Bois, William Edward Burghardt. *The Souls of Black Folk* (Oxford World Classics Edition). Oxford and New York: Oxford University Press, 2007.

Duggan, Lisa. "Queering the State." *Social Text* 39 (1994): 1–14.

Duggan, Lisa, and Nan D. Hunter. *Sex Wars: Sexual Dissent and Political Culture*, 2nd edition. New York: Routledge, 2006.

Dunn, Charles W., and Edward T Byrnes. *Middle English Literature*. London: Routledge, 2013.

Dyer, Richard, ed. *Gays and Film*. London: British Film Institute, 1977.

Ede, Lisa, and Andrea Lunsford. "Audience Addressed/Audience Invoked: The Role of Audience in Composition Theory and Pedagogy." *College Composition and Communication* 35, no. 2 (May 1984): 155–171.

Edwards, Brent Hayes. "The Uses of Diaspora." *Social Text* 66 (2001): 45–73.

Emerson, Ralph Waldo. "The Poet." In *Norton Anthology of Theory and Criticism*, 2nd edition, edited by Vincent B. Leitch, 620–635. 2nd ed. New York: Norton, 2010.

Emerson, Ralph Waldo. *Self-Reliance and Other Essays* (Dover Thrift Editions). New York: Dover Publications, 1993.

Esenwein, J. Berg. *Writing the Short-Story; A Practical Handbook on the Rise, Structure, Writing, and Sale of the Modern Short-Story*. New York: Hinds, Hayden & Eldridge, 1918.

Ewick, Patricia, and Susan S Silbey. "Conformity, Contestation, and Resistance: An Account of Legal Consciousness." *New England Law Review* 26 (1992): 731–749.

Fanon, Frantz. *Black Skin, White Masks*. New York: Grove Press, 2008.

Feagin, Joe R., and Clarence B. Feagin. *Discrimination American Style: Institutional Racism and Sexism*. Malabar: Robert E. Krieger, 1984.

Ferguson, Roderick A. "Reading Intersectionality." In *Race, Gender, Sexuality, and Social Class: Dimensions of Inequality*. Thousand Oaks, CA: Sage, 2012.

Fish, Stanley. *Is There a Text in This Class? The Authority of Interpretive Communities*. Cambridge, MA: Harvard University Press, 1982.

Fortenbaugh, W. W. *Aristotle on Emotion*, 2nd edition. London: Duckworth, 2002.

Fortier, Anne-Marie. "Re-membering Places and the Performance of Belonging(s)." *Theory, Culture & Society* 16, no. 2 (1999): 41–64.

Foucault, Michel. *Foucault Live: (Interviews, 1961–1984)*, translated by Lysa Hochroth and John Johnston, edited by Sylvère Lotringer. New York: Semiotext(e), 1996.

Foucault, Michel. *The History of Sexuality, Volume 1: An Introduction*. New York: Pantheon Books, 1978.

Foucault, Michel. *The History of Sexuality. Vol. 1, An Introduction*, translated by R. Hurley. New York: Random House, 1990.

Foucault, Michel. *Power/Knowledge: Selected Interviews and Other Writings, 1972–1977*. New York: Vintage Books, 1980.

Foucault, Michel. "*Society Must Be Defended*": *Lectures at the Collège De France, 1975–76*. London: Macmillan Publishers, 2003.

Foucault, Michel. "What Is an Author?" In *Critical Theory since 1965*, edited by Hazard Adams and Leroy Searle, 137–148. Essay translated by Donald F. Bouchard and Sherry Simon. Tallahassee: University Presses of Florida / Florida State University Press, 1986.

Foucault, Michel. "What Is an Author?" In *The Book History Reader*, edited by David Finkelstein and Alistair McCleery, 225–231. London: Routledge, 2002.

Fraser, Nancy. "Rethinking Recognition." *New Left Review* 3 (2000): 107.

Freud, Sigmund. "Group Psychology and the Analysis of the Ego [1921]," translated by James Strachey. *The Standard Edition of the Complete Psychological Works of Sigmund Freud*, vol. 18, 65–144. London: Hogarth, 1955.

Fuchs, Stephan. *Against Essentialism: A Theory of Culture and Society*. Cambridge, MA: Harvard University Press, 2009.

Fuss, Diana. *Essentially Speaking: Feminism, Nature and Difference*. New York: Routledge, 2013.

Gallagher, Charles A. "Color-Blind Privilege: The Social and Political Functions of Erasing the Color Line in Post-Race America." *Race, Gender & Class* 10, no. 4 (2003): 22–37.

Gallardo, Miguel E. *Developing Cultural Humility: Embracing Race, Privilege and Power*. Los Angeles, CA: Sage, 2014.

Gandhi, Leela. *Affective Communities: Anticolonial Thought, Fin-De-Siècle Radicalism, and the Politics of Friendship*. Durham, NC: Duke University Press, 2006.

Garber, Marjorie. "Compassion." In *Compassion: The Culture and Politics of an Emotion*, edited by Lauren Berlant, 15–27. New York: Routledge, 2004.

Gilmore, Ruth Wilson. *Golden Gulag: Prisons, Surplus, Crisis, and Opposition in Globalizing California*. Berkeley: University of California Press, 2007.

Gilroy, Paul. *The Black Atlantic: Modernity and Double Consciousness*. Cambridge, MA: Harvard University Press, 1993.

Goffman, Erving. 1959. *The Presentation of Self in Everyday Life*. New York: Anchor Books.

Goldberg, J., M. Moon, and E. K. Sedgwick. *After Sex?: On Writing since Queer Theory*. Durham, NC: Duke University Press, 2010.

Goldsmith, Kenneth. *Uncreative Writing: Managing Language in the Digital Age*. New York: Columbia University Press, 2011.

Gopinath, Gayatri. *Impossible Desires: Queer Diasporas and South Asian Public Cultures*. Durham, NC: Duke University Press, 2005.

Gordimer, Nadine. *Telling Times: Writing and Living, 1950–2008*. London: Bloomsbury, 2010.

Gordon, Avery. *Keeping Good Time: Reflections on Knowledge, Power, and People*. Boulder, CO: Paradigm Publishing, 2004.

Graham, Julie. "Theory and Essentialism in Marxist Geography." *Antipode* 22, no. 1 (1990): 53–66.

Gramsci, Antonio. *Selections from the Prison Notebooks*. New York: International Publishers, 1971.

Gregg, Melissa, and Gregory J. Seigworth, eds. *The Affect Theory Reader*. Durham, NC: Duke University Press, 2010.

Griffiths, Paul E. *What Emotions Really Are: The Problem of Psychological Categories*. Chicago, IL: University of Chicago Press, 1997.

Halfe, Louise. *Blue Marrow*. Regina: Couteau, 2004.

Hall, Stuart. "Cultural Identity and Diaspora." In *Diaspora and Visual Culture*, 35–47. New York: Routledge, 2014.

Hall, Stuart. "Culture, Community, Nation." *Cultural Studies* 7, no. 3 (1993): 349–363.

Hall, Stuart. "Foucault: Power, Knowledge and Discourse." In *Discourse Theory and Practice: A Reader*, edited by Margaret Wetherell, Stephanie Taylor, and Simeon J. Yates. London: Sage, 2001.

Hall, Stuart. *Race: The Floating Signifier*. Northampton: Media Education Foundation, 1996.

Hall, Stuart. *Representation: Cultural Representations and Signifying Practices*. Thousand Oaks, CA: Sage, 1997.

Harmon, Kristen C., and Jennifer L. Nelson, eds. *Deaf American Prose, 1980–2010*. Washington, DC: Gallaudet University Press, 2012.

Hartley, Jenny. *The Reading Groups Book*. London: Oxford University Press, 2001.

Hays, Pamela A. "Finding a Place in the Multicultural Revolution." In *Developing Cultural Humility: Embracing Race, Privilege and Power*, edited by Miguel E. Gallardo, 49–65. Los Angeles, CA: Sage, 2014.

Heller, Ben A. "Césaire, Aimé." In *Encyclopedia of Latin American and Caribbean Literature, 1900–2003*, edited by Daniel Balderston et al., 128–130. London: Routledge.

Hemphill, Prentice. "Healing Justice Is How We Can Sustain Black Lives." *Huffington Post*. February 7, 2017. Accessed June 18, 2018. Web. https://www.huffingtonpost.com/entry/healing-justice_us_5899e8ade4b0c1284f282ffe

Herbert, Steve. "The Trapdoor of Community." *Annals of the Association of American Geographers* 95, no. 4 (2005): 850–865.

Hevey, David. *The Creatures Time Forgot: Photography and Disability Imagery*. London: Routledge, 1992.

Hogan, Patrick Colm. *Affective Narratology: The Emotional Structure of Stories*. Lincoln: University of Nebraska Press, 2011.

Holpuch, Amanda. "Black Patients Half as Likely to Receive Pain Medication as White Patients, Study Finds." *The Guardian*. August 10, 2016. Accessed June 18, 2018. Web. https://www.theguardian.com/science/2016/aug/10/black-patients-bias-prescriptions-pain-management-medicine-opioids

Hong, Cathy Park. "Delusions of Whiteness in the Avant-Garde." *Lana Turner* 7 (2014). Accessed February 12, 2017. Web. http://www.lanaturnerjournal.com/

hooks, bell. *Belonging: A Culture of Place*. New York: Routledge, 2009.

hooks, bell. *Black Looks: Race and Representation*. Boston, MA: South End Press, 1992.

hooks, bell. "Postmodern Blackness." *Postmodern Culture* 1, no. 1 (1990).

hooks, bell. *Talking Back: Thinking Feminist, Thinking Black*. Boston, MA: South End Press, 1989.

hooks, bell. *Where We Stand: Class Matters*. New York: Routledge, 2000.

Horace. "Ars Poetica," In *The Norton Anthology of Theory and Criticism*, 2nd edition, edited by Vincent B. Leitch, 131. New York: Norton, 2010.

Hughey, M. W. "Racializing Redemption, Reproducing Racism: The Odyssey of Magical Negroes and White Saviors." *Sociology Compass* 6, no. 9 (2012): 751–767.

Hugo, Richard. *The Triggering Town: Lectures and Essays on Poetry and Writing*, 2nd edition. New York: Norton, 2010.

Hull, Gloria T., Patricia Bell Scott, and Barbara Smith. *All the Women Are White, All the Men Are Black, But Some of Us Are Brave*. Old Westbury, NY: Feminist Press, (1982).

Hurston, Zora Neale. *Mules and Men*, Reprint edition. New York: Harper Perennial Modern Classics, 2008.

Husserl, Edmund. *Ideas Pertaining to a Pure Phenomenology and to a Phenomenological Philosophy, Book One*. The Hague: Maritnus Nujhoff Publishers, 1983.

Irvine, Judith T. "Registering Affect: Heteroglossia in the Linguistic Expression of Emotion." In *Language and the Politics of Emotion*, edited by Lila Abu-Lughod and Catherine A. Lutz, 126–161. Cambridge: Cambridge University Press, 1990.

Jackson, Chris. "Widening the Gates: Why Publishing Needs Diversity." In *What Editors Do: The Art, Craft, and Business of Book Editing*, edited by Peter Ginna, 223–230. Chicago: University of Chicago Press, 2017.

Jaggar, Alison M. "Love and Knowledge: Emotion in Feminist Epistemology." In *Women and Reason*, edited by Elizabeth D. Harvey and Kathleen Okruhlik, 115–142. Ann Arbor: University of Michigan Press, 1992.

James, Henry. "The Art of Fiction." In *The Norton Anthology of Theory & Criticism*, 2nd edition, edited by Vincent B. Leitch, 744–759. New York: Norton, 2010.

Jameson, Fredric. "Third-World Literature in the Era of Multinational Capitalism." *Social Text* 15 (Autumn 1986): 65–88.

JanMohamed, Abdul, and David Lloyd, eds. *The Nature and Context of Minority Discourse*. Oxford: Oxford University Press, 1991.

Johnson, Allan G. "The Social Construction of Difference." In *Readings for Diversity and Social Justice*, 3rd edition, edited by Maurianne Adams, Warren J. Blumenfeld, Heather W., Hackman, Madeline L. Peters, and Ximena Zuniga, 15–21. New York: Routledge, 2013.

Johnson, E. Patrick. *Appropriating Blackness: Performance and the Politics of Authenticity*. Durham, NC: Duke University Press, 2003.

Johnson, E. Patrick, and Mae G. Henderson. *Black Queer Studies: A Critical Anthology*. Durham, NC: Duke University Press Books, 2005.

Johnson, John. "Automaticity to Authenticity: Efforts to Prevent Student Misgendering." Presentation at Sacramento State University, Center for Teaching and Learning. May 4, 2018.

Joseph, Miranda. *Against the Romance of Community*. Minneapolis: University of Minnesota Press, 2002.

Joseph, Miranda. "A Debt to Society." In *The Seductions of Community: Emancipations, Oppressions, Quandaries*, edited by Gerald Creed, 199–226. Santa Fe, NM: School for Advanced Research Press, 2006.

Joseph, Miranda. "Community." In *Keywords for American Cultural Studies*, edited by Bruce Burgett and Glen Hendler, 57–59. New York: New York University Press, 2007.

Kafer, Alison. *Feminist, Queer, Crip*. Bloomington: Indiana University Press, 2013.

Keating, AnaLouise. *Transformation Now!: Toward a Post-Oppositional Politics of Change*. Urbana: University of Illinois Press, 2013.

Keeshig-Tobias, Lenore. "Stop Stealing Native Stories." In *Borrowed Power: Essays on Cultural Appropriation*, edited by Bruce Ziff and Pratima V. Rao, 71–74. New Brunswick, NJ: Rutgers, 1997.

Kelley, Robin D.G. "Introduction: What Did Cedric Robinson Mean by Racial Capitalism." In Walter Rodney and Robin D.G. Kelley, "Race Capitalism Justice." *Boston Review: A Political and Literary Journal,* Forum I (2017): 5–8.

Kelley, Robin D. G. "A Poetics of Anticolonialism." *Monthly Review: An Independent Social Magazine* 51, no. 06 (November 1999). Accessed October 7, 2018. Web. https://monthlyreview.org/1999/11/01/a-poetics-of-anticolonialism/

Kerschbaum, Stephanie. *Toward a New Rhetoric of Difference*. Urbana, OH: National Council of Teachers of English, 2014.

Kipling, Rudyard. "The White Man's Burden: The United States and the Philippine Islands." In *Kipling's Verse: Definitive Edition*. New York: Doubleday, 1940.

Klahn, Norma. "Literary (Re)Mappings: Autobiographical (Dis)Placements by Chicana Writers." In *Chicana Feminisms: A Critical Reader*, edited by Gabriela F. Arredondo, et al., 114–146. Durham, NC: Duke University Press, 2003.

Konstan, David. *Pity Transformed*. London: Duckworth, 2001.

Langstraat, Lisa. "The Point Is There Is No Point: Miasmic Cynicism and Cultural Studies Composition." *JAC: Journal of Advanced Composition* 22, no. 2 (2002): 293–325.

Larsen, Nella. *Passing*. New York: Modern Library, 2007.

Leys, Ruth. "The Turn to Affect: A Critique." *Critical Inquiry* 37, no. 3: 434–472.

Little, Adrian. *The Politics of Community: Theory and Practice*. Edinburgh: Edinburgh University Press, 2002.

Longinus. *On the Sublime*, translated by W. H. Fyfe. Revised by Donald Russell. Cambridge, MA: Harvard University Press, 1995.

Lorde, Audre. *Sister Outsider: Essays and Speeches*. Berkeley, CA: The Crossing Press, 1984.

Lowe, Lisa. "The Intimacies of Four Continents." In *Haunted By Empire: Geographies of Intimacy in North American History*, edited by Ann Laura Stoler, Durham, NC: Duke University Press Books, 2006.

Lugones, María. "Hablando Cara a Cara / Speaking Face to Face: An Exploration of Ethnocentric Racism." In *Making Face, Making Soul/Haciendo Caras: Creative and Critical Perspectives by Feminists of Color*, edited by Gloria Anzaldúa, 46–55. San Francisco, CA: Aunt Lute Books, 1995.

Lugones, María. *Pilgrimages/Peregrinajes: Theorizing Coalition against Multiple Oppressions (Feminist Constructions)*. New York: Rowman, 2003.

Lukács, Georg. *History and Class Consciousness: Studies in Marxist Dialectics*. Cambridge: MIT Press, 1967.

Lutz, Catherine A., and Lila Abu-Lughod, eds. *Language and the Politics of Emotion*. Cambridge: Cambridge University Press, 1990.

Lyotard, Jean-François. *The Postmodern Condition: A Report on Knowledge*, translated by Geoff Bennington and Brian Massumi. Minneapolis: University of Minnesota Press, 1979.

Malkki, Liisa. "National Geographic: The Rooting of Peoples and the Territorialization of National Identity among Scholars and Refugees." *Cultural Anthropology* 7, no. 1 (February 1992): 24–44.

Marx, Karl. *Capital: A Critique of Political Economy*, V.I. Middlesex: Penguin, 1976.

Marx, Karl. "Contribution to the Critique of Hegel's Philosophy of Law." In *Critique of Hegel's Philosophy of Right*, translated by Joseph O'Malley, transcribed by Andy Blunden. Oxford: Oxford University Press, 1970. Web. www.marxists.org/archive

Maslow, Abraham Harold. "A Theory of Human Motivation." *Psychological Review* 50, no. 4 (1943): 370.

Massumi, Brian. *Parables for the Virtual: Movement, Affect, Sensation*. Durham, NC: Duke University Press, 2002.

McCann, Carole, and Seung-kyung Kim. *Feminist Theory Reader: Local and Global Perspectives*, 2nd edition. London: Routledge, 2010.

McClintock, Anne. *Imperial Leather: Race, Gender, and Sexuality in the Colonial Contest*. New York: Routledge, 1995.

McGurl, Mark. *The Program Era: Postwar Fiction and the Rise of Creative Writing*. Boston, MA: Harvard University Press, 2009.

McIntosh, Peggy. "White Privilege and Male Privilege: A Personal Account of Coming to See Correspondences through Work in Women's Studies." Working Paper 189. Wellesley College Center for Research on Women, 1988.

McLeod, Neal, ed. *Indigenous Poetics in Canada*. Waterloo, IA: Wilfrid Laurier University Press, 2014.

McWhorter, Ladelle. "Culture or Nature? The Function of the Term 'Body' in the Work of Michel Foucault." *The Journal of Philosophy* 86, no. 11 (1989): 608–614.

Mercredi, Duncan. "Achimo." In *Indigenous Poetics in Canada*, edited by Neal McLeod, 17–23. Waterloo, IA: Wilfrid Laurier University Press, 2014.

Merleau-Ponty, Maurice. *Phenomenology of Perception*. London: Routledge, 2013.

Mill, John Stuart. "Thoughts on Poetry and Its Varieties." *The Crayon* 7, no. 4 (1860): 93–97.

Milton, Kay. "Meanings, Feelings, and Human Ecology." In *Mixed Emotions: Anthropological Studies of Feeling*, edited by Kay Milton and Maruška Svašek, 25–41. Oxford: Berg, 2005.

Minot, Stephen. *Three Genres: The Writing of Poetry, Fiction, and Drama*, 7th edition. Upper Saddle River, NJ: Prentice Hall, 2003.

Mogul, Joey, Andrea Ritchie, and Kay Whitlock. *Queer (In)Justice: The Criminalization of LGBT People in the United States*. Boston, MA: Beacon Press, 2011.

Moldoveanu, Mihnea, and Nitin Nohria, eds. *Master Passions: Emotion, Narrative, and the Development of Culture*. Cambridge, MA: MIT Press, 2002.

Morgan, Cheryl. "Writing Better Trans Characters." September 28, 2015. Accessed April 1, 2019. Web. http://strangehorizons.com/non-fiction/articles/writing-better-trans-characters/

Morrison, Toni. "A Humanist View." Speech, Portland State University. May 30, 1975. Transcribed by Keisha E. McKenzie. Accessed June 18, 2018. Web. https://mackenzian.com/blog/2014/07/07/transcript-morrison-1975/

Morrison, Toni. Interview with Bill Moyers. March 11, 1990. Accessed June 18, 2018. Web. https://billmoyers.com/content/toni-morrison

Morrison, Toni. *Playing in the Dark: Whiteness and the Literary Imagination.* New York: Vintage Books, 1993.

Morton, Donald, and Mas'ud Zavarzadeh. "The Cultural Politics of the Fiction Workshop." *Cultural Critique* 11 (Winter 1988–1989): 155–173.

Nafisi, Azar. *Reading Lolita in Tehran: A Memoir in Books.* London: Harper Collins, 2004.

Neuhaus, Mareike. *The Decolonizing Poetics of Indigenous Literatures.* Regina: University of Regina Press, 2015.

Ng, Roxana. "Toward an Embodied Pedagogy: Exploring Health and the Body through Chinese Medicine." In *Indigenous Knowledges in Global Contexts: Multiple Readings of Our World*, edited by George J. Sefa Dei, Budd L. Hall, and Dorothy Goldin Rosenberg, 168–183. Toronto: University of Toronto Press, 2000.

Nguyen, Viet Thanh. "How Writers' Workshops Can Be Hostile." *New York Times.* April 27, 2017. Accessed February 2, 2018. Web. https://www.nytimes.com/2017/04/26/.../viet-thanh-nguyen-writers-workshops.html

Ni, Zhange. "Postsecular Reading." In *The Cambridge Companion to Literature and Religion*, edited by Susan M. Felch, 51–69. New York: Cambridge University Press, 2016.

Northen, Michael. "A Short History of American Disability Poetry." In *Beauty Is a Verb: The New Poetry of Disability*, edited by Jennifer Bartlett, Sheila Black, and Michael Northen, 18–27. El Paso, TX: Cinco Puntos, 2011.

Nussbaum, Martha Craven. *Upheavals of Thought: The Intelligence of Emotions.* Cambridge, UK: Cambridge University Press, 1991.

Older, Daniel José. "Diversity Is Not Enough: Race, Power, Publishing." In *Literary Publishing in the Twenty-First Century*, edited by Travis Kurowski, Wayne Miller, and Kevin Prufer, 154–165. Minneapolis, MN: Milkweed, 2016.

Omi, Michael, and Howard Winant. *Racial Formation in the United States*, 3rd edition. London: Routledge, 2015.

Ong, Walter. "The Writer's Audience Is Always a Fiction." *PMLA* 90, no. 1 (January 1975): 9–21.

Pateman, Trevor. "Writing: Some Thoughts on the Teachable and Unteachable in Creative Writing." *Journal of Aesthetic Education* 32, no. 3 (Fall 1998): 83–90.

Pelli, Denis G., and Charles Bigelow. "A Writing Revolution." *Seed Magazine.* 2009. Accessed October 24, 2018. Web. http://seedmagazine.com/content/article/a_writing_revolution/

Pérez-Torres, Rafael. *Movements in Chicano Poetry: Against Myths, against Margins.* Cambridge, UK: Cambridge University Press, 1915.

Philip, M. NourbeSe. "The Disappearing Debate: Or How the Discussion of Racism Has Been Taken Over by the Censorship Issue." In *Borrowed Power:*

Essays on Cultural Appropriation, edited by Bruce Ziff and Pratima V. Rao, 97–109. New Brunswick, NJ: Rutgers, 1997.

Piepzna-Samarasinha, Leah Lakshmi. "A Not-So-Brief Personal History of the Healing Justice Movement, 2010–2016." *MICE*, no. 2 (2016). Accessed June 18, 2018. Web. http://micemagazine.ca/issue-two/not-so-brief-personal-history-healing-justice-movement-2010%E2%80%932016

Ponterotto, Joseph G., and Eduardo Duran. *Finding My Cultural Selves: The Journey Continues*. In *Developing Cultural Humility: Embracing Race, Privilege and Power*, edited by Miguel E. Gallardo, 27–49. Los Angeles, CA: Sage, 2014.

Povinelli, Elizabeth A. *Economies of Abandonment: Social Belonging and Endurance in Late Liberalism*. Durham, NC: Duke University Press, 2011.

Protevi, John. *Political Affect: Connecting the Social and the Somatic*. Minneapolis: University of Minnesota Press, 2009.

Puar, Jasbir. *Terrorist Assemblages: Homonationalism in Queer Times*. Durham, NC: Duke University Press Books, 2007.

Rankine, Camille. "What's in a Number." *Medium: Nat. Brut*. August 22, 2015. Accessed November 20, 2018. Web. https://medium.com/nat-brut/what-s-in-a-number-cc4f12e1718d

Rankine, Claudia, Beth Loffreda, and Max King Cap, eds. *The Racial Imaginary: Writers on Race in the Life of the Mind*. Albany, NY: Fence, 2015.

Rifkin, Mark. *Settler Common Sense: Queerness and Everyday Colonialism in the American Renaissance*. Minneapolis: University of Minnesota Press, 2014.

Riley, Denise. *Impersonal Passion: Language as Affect*. Durham, NC: Duke University Press, 2005.

Robertson, Roland. *European Glocalization in Global Context*. New York: Palgrave Macmillan, 2014.

Robinson, Cedric J. *Black Marxism: The Making of the Black Radical Tradition*. Chapel Hill and London: University of North Carolina Press, 1983.

Rodney, Walter. *How Europe Underdeveloped Africa*. Baltimore: Black Classic Press, 2011.

Rousseau, Jean-Jacques. *The Social Contract and the First and Second Discourses*, edited by Susan Dunn. New Haven: Yale University Press, 2002.

Rushdie, Salman. *Imaginary Homelands: Essays and Criticism 1981–1991*. New York: Random House, 2012.

Russ, Joanna. "What Can a Heroine Do? Or Why Women Can't Write." In *Images of Women in Fiction; Feminist Perspectives*, edited by Susan Koppelman Cornillon, 3–20. Bowling Green, OH: Bowling Green University Popular Press, 1972.

Rutherford, Jonathan. *Identity: Community, Culture, Difference*. London, UK: Lawrence & Wishart, 1990.

Said, Edward. *Culture and Imperialism*. New York: Vintage Books, 1994.

Salesses, Matthew. "We Need Diverse Diverse Books." *LitHub*. August 31, 2015. Accessed November 20, 2018. Web. https://lithub.com/we-need-diverse-diverse-books/

Sánchez, Elba Rosario. "*Cartohistografía: Continente de una voz /* Cartohistography: One Voice's Continent." In *Chicana Feminisms: A Critical Reader*, edited by Gabriela F. Arredondo, et al. Durham, NC: Duke University Press, 2003.

Sanders, Julie. *Adaptation and Appropriation: The New Critical Idiom*. New York: Routledge, 2016.

Sandoval, Chela. *Methodology of the Oppressed*. Minneapolis: University of Minnesota Press, 2000.

Sandoval, Chela. "US Third World Feminism: The Theory and Method of Oppositional Consciousness in the Postmodern World." *Genders* 10 (1991): 1–24.

Schalk, Sami. *Bodyminds Reimagined: (Dis)ability, Race, and Gender in Black Women's Speculative Fiction*. Durham, NC: Duke University Press, 2018.

Scott, Joan W. *Gender and the Politics of History*. New York: Columbia University Press, 1988.

Scott, Joan W. "Gender: A Useful Category of Historical Analysis." *The American Historical Review* 91, no. 5 (1986): 1053–1075.

Sedgwick, Eve Kosofsky. *Touching Feeling: Affect, Pedagogy, Performativity*. Durham, NC: Duke University Press, 2003.

Selasi, Taiye. "Stop Pigeonholing African Writers." *The Guardian*. July 4, 2015. Accessed June 18, 2018. Web. https://www.theguardian.com/books/2015/jul/04/taiye-selasi-stop-pigeonholing-african-writers

Sellers, Robert M., et al. "Multidimensional Inventory of Black Identity: A Preliminary Investigation of Reliability and Construct Validity." *Journal of Personality and Social Psychology* 73, no. 4 (1997): 805–815.

Sethi, Rita Chaudhry. "Smells Like Racism." In *Race, Class, and Gender in the United States: An Integrated Study*, 9th edition, edited by Paula S. Rothenberg, 140–147. New York: Worth, 2013.

Shelby, Tommie. *We Who Are Dark: The Philosophical Foundations of Black Solidarity*. Cambridge, MA: Harvard University Press, 2007.

Shelley, Percy Bysshe. "From a Defense of Poetry. Or Remarks Suggested by an Essay Entitled 'the Four Ages of Poetry.'" In *Norton Anthology of Theory and Criticism*, 2nd edition, edited by Vincent B. Leitch, 620–635. 2nd ed. New York: Norton, 2010.

Siebers, Tobin Anthony. *Disability Aesthetics*. Ann Arbor: University of Michigan Press, 2010.

Siegel, Ben, ed. *The American Writer and the University*. Newark: University of Delaware Press; Associated University Presses, 1989.

Smith, Adam. *The Theory of Moral Sentiments*, edited by Ryan Patrick Hanley. New York: Penguin, 2009. First published by A. Millar, London and A. Kincaid and J. Bell, Edinburgh, 1759.

Smith, Andrea. *Conquest: Sexual Violence and American Indian Genocide*. Boston, MA: South End Press, 2005.

Smith, Barbara Herrnstein. *Contingencies of Value: Alternative Perspectives for Critical Theory*. Cambridge, MA: Harvard University Press, 1988.

Solomon, Robert C., ed. *What Is an Emotion? Classic and Contemporary Readings*, 2nd edition. Oxford: Oxford University Press, 2003.

Somerville, Siobhan B. "Queer." In Burgett, B., and Hendler, G. *Keywords for American Cultural Studies*. New York: New York University Press, 2007.

Somerville, Siobhan B. *Queering the Color Line: Race and the Invention of Homosexuality in American Culture*. Durham, NC: Duke University Press Books, 1999.

Sommer, Doris. *Proceed with Caution, When Engaged by Minority Writing in the Americas*. Cambridge, MA: Harvard University Press, 1999.

Spade, Dean, and Craig Willse. "Norms and Normalization." In *The Oxford Handbook of Feminist Theory*, edited by Lisa Disch and Mary Hawkesworth, New York: Oxford University Press, 2016.

Spivak, Gayatri. "'Criticism, Feminism, and the Institution': Interview with Elizabeth Grosz." *Thesis Eleven* 10, no. 11 (November/March 1984–5): 175–187.

Stegner, Manfred B. *Globalization: A Very Short Introduction*. London: Oxford University Press, 2017.

Stine, Alison. "On Poverty." *Kenyon Review*. February 29, 2016. Accessed June 18, 2018. Web. https://www.kenyonreview.org/2016/02/on-poverty/

Stoler, Ann Laura. "Intimidations of Empire: Predicaments of the Tactile and Unseen." In *Haunted By Empire: Geographies of Intimacy in North American History*, edited by Ann Laura Stoler, Durham, NC: Duke University Press Books, 2006.

Stygall, Gail. "Resisting Privilege: Basic Writing and Foucault's Author Function." *College Composition and Communication* 45, no. 3 (October 1994): 320–341.

Sudbury, Julia. "From the Point of No Return to the Women's Prison: Writing Spaces of Confinement into Diaspora Studies." *Canadian Woman Studies* 23, no. 2 (2004): 154–163.

Summerfield, Judith. "'Is There a Life in This Text?' Reimagining Narrative." In *Writing Theory and Critical Theory*, edited by John Clifford and John Schilb, 179–195. New York: MLA, 1994.

Svašek, Maruška. "Introduction: Emotion in Anthropology." In *Mixed Emotions: Anthropological Studies of Feeling*, edited by Kay Milton and Maruška Svašek. Oxford: Berg, 2005.

Svašek, Maruška. "The Politics of Chosen Trauma: Expellee Memories, Emotions and Identities." In *Mixed Emotions: Anthropological Studies of Feeling*, edited by Kay Milton and Maruška Svašek, 195–214. Oxford: Berg, 2005.

Sy, Waaseyaa'sin Christine. "Through Iskigamizigan (The Sugarbush): A Poetics of Decolonization." In *Indigenous Poetics in Canada*, edited by Neal McLeod, 183–203. Waterloo, IA: Wilfrid Laurier University Press, 2014.

Tatum, Beverly Daniel. "The Complexity of Identity: 'Who Am I?'" In *Readings for Diversity and Social Justice*, 3rd edition, edited by Maurianne Adams, Warren J. Blumenfeld, Heather W. Hackman, Madeline L. Peters, and Ximena Zuniga, 6–9. New York: Routledge, 2013.

Taylor, Astra, dir. *Examined Life*. 2009. New York City: Zeitgeist Films.

Terdiman, Richard. *Discourse/Counter-Discourse: The Theory and Practice of Symbolic Resistance in Nineteenth-Century France*. Ithaca, NY: Cornell University Press, 1989.

Tervalon, M., and J. Murray-Garcia. "Cultural Humility Versus Cultural Competence: A Critical Distinction in Defining Physician Training Outcomes in Multicultural Education." *Journal of Health Care for the Poor and Underserved* 9, no. 2 (1998): 117–125.

Thomsen, Mads Rosendahl. *Mapping World Literature: International Canonization and Transnational Literatures*. London: Continuum, 2008.

Tolstoy, Leo. *What Is Art?* New York: Penguin, 1995.

Tomkins, Silvan S. *Exploring Affect: The Selected Writings of Silvan S Tomkins*, edited by E. Virginia Demos. Cambridge: Cambridge University Press, 1995.

Toomer, Jean. *Cane*. New York: WW Norton & Company, 1993.

Trautwein, Catherine. "Women Writers Are Over Hearing These Sexist Comments." *Time Magazine*. April 18, 2017. Accessed October 28, 2018. Web. http://time.com/4744640/things-only-women-writers-hear-highlights-sexism/

Trinh Minh-ha. *When the Moon Waxes Red: Representation, Gender, and Cultural Politics*. New York: Routledge, 1991.

Tuck, Eve, and K. Wayne Yang. "Decolonization Is Not a Metaphor." *Decolonization: Indigeneity, Education & Society* 1, no. 1 (2012): 1–40.

VIDA: Women in Literary Arts. *VIDA Count*. Accessed June 18, 2018. Web. www.vidaweb.org.

Wallis, Brian. "Black Bodies, White Science: The Slave Daguerreotypes of Louis Agassiz." *The Journal of Blacks in Higher Education*, no. 12 (Summer, 1996): 102–106.

Wang, Dorothy J. *Thinking Its Presence: Form, Race, and Subjectivity in Contemporary Asian American Poetry*. Stanford, CA: Stanford University Press, 2013.

Weber, Max. *Economy and Society*. Berkeley: University of California Press, 1978.

Wesling, Meg. "Why Queer Diaspora?" *Feminist Review* 90, no. 1 (2008): 30–47.

Williams, Raymond. *Keywords: A Vocabulary of Culture and Society, New Edition*. Oxford and New York: Oxford University Press, 2015.

Willoughby-Herard, Tiffany. "Abolition and Kinship." *Abolition: A Journal of Insurgent Politics*. 2016. Accessed May 25 2016. Web. https://abolitionjournal.org/abolition-and-kinship/

Winchester, Caleb Thomas. *Some Principles of Literary Criticism*. New York: The Macmillan Company, 1905.

Wittig, Monique. *The Straight Mind and Other Essays*. Boston, MA: Beacon Press, 1992.

Wordsworth, William. "Preface to Lyrical Ballads, with Pastoral and Other Poems [1802]." In *Norton Anthology of Theory and Criticism*, edited by Vincent B. Leitch, et al. New York: Norton, 2010.

Young, Iris Marion. "Five Faces of Oppression." In *Readings for Diversity and Social Justice*, 3rd edition, edited by Maurianne Adams, Warren J. Blumenfeld, Heather W. Hackman, Madeline L. Peters, and Ximena Zuniga, 35–45. New York: Routledge, 2013.

Young, John K. *Black Writers, White Publishers: Marketplace Politics in Twentieth-Century African American Literature*. Jackson: University Press of Mississippi, 2010.

Young, Robert. *Colonial Desire: Hybridity in Theory, Culture and Race*. London: Routledge, 1995.

Yúdice, George. "Marginality and the Ethics of Survival." *Social Text* 21 (1989): 214–236.

Yuval-Davis, Nira. "Belonging and the Politics of Belonging." *Patterns of Prejudice* 40, no. 3 (2006): 197–214.

Yuval-Davis, Nira. *The Politics of Belonging: Intersectional Contestations*. London: Sage, 2011.

Ziff, Bruce, and Pratima V. Rao. *Borrowed Power: Essays on Cultural Appropriation*. New Brunswick, NJ: Rutgers, 1997.

Zinn, Howard. *You Can't Be Neutral on a Moving Train: A Personal History of Our Times*. Boston, MA: Beacon Press, 2002.

INDEX